But How Can I?

But How Can I?

by

Doris Black

and

Charlotte Mize

21ˢᵗ CENTURY CHRISTIAN

NASHVILLE, TENNESSEE

But How Can I?

Published in 1998 by 21st Century Christian,
2809 Granny White Pike, Nashville, TN 37204

Cover Design: a.k.a. graphic design

ISBN: 0-89098-204-X

Printed in the U.S.A.

Dedicated

to

*Our spiritual family in Tempe, Arizona
without whom this book would have never
been written,*

to

*Our spiritual family in Round Rock, Texas
without whom this book would have never
been published,*

to

God who brought it all together.

Contents

"You Haven't Told Me How"

"You tell me my attitude is wrong, and I know that is true, but you haven't told me how to change it," wailed our 14 year-old daughter in frustration. My mind flashed to the countless lessons I had heard censuring ingratitude and selfishness (two attitudes she had been displaying), yet I had never heard a lesson that taught how to change a *wrong* attitude into a *right* one. I recalled times in my own life when I had felt envious and hated myself for it, yet had been unable to erase that envy from my heart.

Does the Word of God only identify sin and condemn it? Does it only offer us forgiveness, freedom from guilt and the promise of redemption or does it teach us in a practical way how to overcome sin in our daily lives?

Paul's words came to mind. *"All scripture is God-breathed and is useful for teaching, rebuking, correcting and training in righteousness, so that the man of God may be thoroughly equipped for every good work."* (2 Timothy 3:16) If we are to be equipped for every good work, then overcoming sinful attitudes and behaviors would be a part of that training. But how do you change an ungrateful heart into a grateful one; a heart filled with resentment and bitterness into one filled with forgiveness and love; an anxious, fearful heart into one of trust and peace; a selfish, self-centered heart to a selfless, self-sacrificing one?

In an attempt to answer these questions, this study was born. We have tried to be practical in dealing with common attitude problems so that, not only is a problem identified and discussed, but a solution is presented to overcome it in daily living.

Our prayer is that these suggestions will be helpful.

1. Anger

"Anyone can become angry. That is easy. But to be angry with the right person, to the right degree, at the right time, for the right purpose and in the right way—that is not easy."

—Aristotle

THE PROBLEM

Have you ever become angry and (1) lashed out verbally or physically just to hurt; (2) sulked and pouted, wallowing in self-pity; (3) made a fool of yourself in a temper tantrum; (4) controlled your behavior but become resentful and bitter? If so, join the human race, you've had a sinful response to anger.

The force and frequency of angry feelings have probably caused more broken hearts, broken homes and broken heads than any other emotion. Angry feelings are like dynamite sticks, useful when managed correctly but they kill, cripple, maim and scar when uncontrolled or handled improperly.

Man's Natural Response to Anger

Man, by nature, responds to anger in two different ways. The first and most dramatic is the explosion, capable of wreaking havoc and leaving paths of destruction. The second is the implosion—internalized anger. It is more subtle and sometimes slower but it can be just as devastating and deadly.

The Explosion

The explosion is easily recognized for it is always accompanied by some type of violent behavior. Though you tend to think of violence as kicking, hitting and gouging, you cannot ignore or

9

dismiss the wounds inflicted by the violent tongue. James 3:6 speaks of this type of violence, *"The tongue also is a fire, a world of evil among the parts of the body. It corrupts the whole person, sets the whole course of his life on fire, and is itself set on fire by hell."*

During an explosion of anger some people who recoil at the thought of bringing physical pain to others may not hesitate to land a barrage of verbal abuse that causes more emotional and mental damage than any physical blow and with more lasting effects.

The explosion usually has one objective—to hurt. Even when that is not the aim, it is usually the result. When it is directed at the object of your anger, it serves as punishment or revenge. When it is directed at the world in general, it serves to make everyone else as miserable as you.

Man usually attempts to justify his explosions with, "Well, they made me mad...Of course I did that, but you should have heard what they said to me...I may have, but I was mad...."

Some schools of behavioral science not only justify anger explosions they encourage them by teaching to go ahead, explode, and:

• *Get it out of your system.* This theory is a fallacy. You can never explode anger out of your system. You may get even, and your anger may be temporarily relieved, but you have not gotten it out of your system. Quite the contrary, each explosion furrows the rut a little deeper for the next angry explosion.

• *You will feel better.* You might, until you realize that no one else does and you have to deal with the mess your explosion has created (the hurt feelings, the broken relationships, the barriers, etc.).

• *Just direct it in a way that does not harm.* This theory teaches to, among other things, pretend a pillow is the object (husband, wife, parent, friend, etc.) of your anger and kick, hit, stab and scream at the pillow until your anger is drained. This theory reasons that by directing the explosion in this way, supposedly it will be harmless. But in essence you are committing mental violence or murder. Jesus condemned sins of the mind in Matthew 5:28. And though you may receive a temporary form of relief

10

because you have *gotten even* in fantasy, you have not dealt with reality. The problem that triggered your angry feelings is still there, ready to trigger them again. In addition, you are establishing dangerous thinking patterns (hit, beat, stab, kill).

Explosions are never harmless, and what is more they do not solve problems. Your temper may brow beat someone into letting you have your way but you have not solved the problem.

Internalized Anger or Seething Mad

Internalized anger is frequently more difficult to recognize than explosive anger even though it is every bit as painful and certainly just as dangerous. It is like a festering boil. The pressure builds in internalized anger and the pain increases until it is no longer bearable, then it erupts into an exploding volcano or a seeping sore of resentment, bitterness and hatred.

Internalized anger has a mental dialogue. And when you hear yourself thinking, "It is not fair...They do this to me all the time...I'll get even if it is the last thing I do...How much longer do I have to take this..," be alert to the peril of unresolved anger in your life.

What Causes Angry Feelings

There are many situations and circumstances that cause angry feelings to flare, but the majority are rooted in James 4:1, *"What causes fights and quarrels among you? Don't they come from your desires that battle within you? You want something but don't get it..."* This base for anger is practiced in a variety of combinations:

- Someone is doing something you don't want them to.
- Someone is not doing something you want them to.
- Someone is doing something in a way you don't want it done.
- Something is not getting done fast enough—or getting done too fast.
- Someone has *offended* or wronged you.
- Someone has violated your *rights*.
- You are frustrated over something you can't change.

Though knowing the cause of angry feelings is often of value, God has given strong warnings concerning anger *regardless of the cause.*

"For man's anger does not bring about the righteous life that God desires." James is telling us in 1:20 that man's anger is a handicap to a righteous life. Which you can attest to as you recall sins you've committed while under the influence of anger.

"A fool gives full vent to his anger, but a wise man keeps himself under control." (Proverbs 29:11) This proverb calls the man who vents his anger a fool. That definitely stands to reason considering it puts him at odds with those around him and with God.

"An angry man stirs up dissension, and a hot-tempered man commits many sins." (Proverbs 29:22) These are two excellent reasons for controlling anger.

THE SOLUTION

If you recognize that you have a problem with anger, then you face a choice. You can be like the blind man in the ninth chapter of John when Jesus offered to heal him. You can obey Jesus and go wash the mud from your eyes and return with spiritual and physical sight, or you can be like the rich young ruler of Matthew 19:22. When Jesus told him of a change he needed to make in his life, *"...he went away sorrowful,"* not willing to make the sacrifice.

Where Do You Start

Any change starts with repentance—repentance that is more than being sorry you've messed up or sorry you've been caught. True repentance is motivated by sorrow for your disobedience to God, for your sinful behavior, and for the pain you have caused. It must be a sorrow that moves you to *want to* change. And with God's training, you can. If your *want to* is weak, spending consistent time in the Bible being confronted by God's teachings will strengthen your *want to* power.

True repentance seeks forgiveness from God and others. In this way you are relieved of feelings of guilt and you give those you have harmed an opportunity to overcome feelings of anger and resentment they may have.

Know That An Angry Feeling Can Work For You

To experience an angry feeling is not sin. There are over 80 occasions in the Old Testament that scripture says, "God was angry." Angry feelings are usually unbidden responses just as happy and sad feelings are usually unbidden. Although we can't always control their coming, we can control our response to them.

Emotions (or feelings) have been given to mankind by God and when managed as He intended, they are good. Most serve to motivate, i.e., passion motivates you to intimacy and reproduction; sorrow motivates you to face the reality of a situation; fear motivates you to be cautious; and anger can motivate you to deal with a problem, whether it be in your environment or your attitude.

For example, consider a squeaking door that should have been fixed long ago. Everytime you hear it, you feel angry or irritated. You can respond to those feelings by (1) yelling and screaming at someone who has not fixed it, though asked many times; you can tear it off the hinges; you can kick the dog and make the kids turn off the cartoons; or (2) you can get a can of oil and fix the door.

In your first response you attacked the world, in the second you attacked the problem.

God's Ideal Method For Handling Anger

The first and most effective of God's methods not only deals with the angry feelings, it prevents most of them. It could be called the *New Man* or *Replacement* method. The basis of this method is taught in Romans 6 where Paul teaches the *old you* was buried in Christ, the *new you* has a new life to live and a new way to behave. Although the angry feelings of the *old you* were usually unbidden they were often triggered by wrong attitudes that should die with you in Christ.

13

Ephesians 4:22-24 gives specific instructions for implementing your new life. Recently scientists have discovered this method which they call Behavior Modification. It teaches you to quit doing one thing by doing something in its place. God has used it for centuries to teach his children to *"quit lying by speaking only the truth"* Ephesians 4:25, *"get rid of your anger, rage, slander, and brawling by being kind, compassionate and forgiving"* Ephesians 4:31-32.

Unfortunately, the sinful patterns of the old you are often stronger than the faith of the new you. But God in his wisdom included some fundamental methods for dealing with anger, until you mature spiritually enough for the *selflessness* of the new you to neutralize the anger of the old you.

Back To The Basics

Using God's basic methods for handling angry feelings is similar to a return to childhood for reprogramming your responses to anger.

The first method we will call the *DROP IT* method. God says in Proverbs 17:14, *"Starting a quarrel is like breaching a dam; so drop the matter before a dispute breaks out."* In other words, shut your mouth, take a walk, mind your own business, do whatever you have to do but "drop it" before the fight starts and you cannot drop it.

A second method is the *HOLD IT* method. It is in direct conflict with man's "Go Ahead and Explode" theory. Proverbs 29:11 says, *"A fool gives full vent to his anger, but a wise man, holding it back quiets it."* (NAS) This does not teach to internalize anger; it teaches to control your anger by holding it back to see if it quiets down.

A third method is the *ARE YOU LISTENING* method. James says in 1:19, *"My dear brothers, take note of this: Everyone should be quick to listen, slow to speak and slow to become angry."* So many angry feelings could be avoided by listening. Many quarrels are the result of assumptions and misunderstandings—someone was not listening.

14

The fourth method could be called the *CLOSE YOUR MOUTH AND THINK* method. Proverbs 15:28 teaches, *"The heart of the righteous weighs its answer, but the mouth of the wicked gushes evil."* A man striving to live righteously will ask himself, "Is what I am going to say true? Is it fair? Will it bring unnecessary pain?" While the person not committed to righteousness just opens his mouth while evil and vicious words roll out.

A fifth way to handle anger is God's *REMOVE YOURSELF FROM A TEMPTING SITUATION* method. God teaches this method by example in Exodus 32 and 33. There God told the Israelites their stubbornness and rebellion provoked him to such anger that he might destroy them; therefore, he would send an angel in his place to guide them on their journey to Canaan. God was not avoiding a problem in this decision. He had already dealt with the immediate problem (making of the golden calf) and had taken steps to prepare them for the future. In the meantime, he was going to remove himself from a situation that would trigger anger in him. Proverbs 22:3 teaches this type of foresight, *"A prudent man sees danger and takes refuge, but the simple keep going and suffer for it."*

A sixth method could be called the *COOL IT* method. Proverbs 15:1 teaches, *"A gentle answer turns away wrath, but a harsh word stirs up anger."* This proverb is often viewed as beautiful poetry without realizing the strength involved. The gentleness of your voice is a dynamic and simple tool for controlling your own anger and the anger of others. The muscles in your body must tense to speak angrily, they must relax to speak gently. Unfortunately, it is easy to develop the habit of speaking with harsh and irritated tones that infect your whole environment with tenseness.

The seventh and ultimate method is the *SPEAKING THE TRUTH IN LOVE* method. If you have tried the basics and you still have angry feelings, not being able to forget or forgive, then you must speak the truth in love. Speaking the truth in love is openly telling the other person of your feelings of anger but in a loving (I Corinthians 13:4-7) manner. If he changes the behavior that is bothering you, then you can rejoice. If he does not, then you must forgive as Paul teaches in Ephesians 4:32 and leave his response in the hands of God. (Romans 12:17-19)

These basic methods are so simple we tend to dismiss them without trial just as Namaan wanted to when God told him to dip in the river Jordan seven times to cure his leprosy. (2 Kings 5:1-27) His young slave pointed out that if God had given him something difficult he would have gone to great lengths to have performed it, so why not put the same energy into something simple God had commanded?

Namaan agreed to try God's way (with some skepticism) and found that the simplicity of God's commands is greater than the difficult is creative imaginations of man.

DISCUSSION QUESTIONS

1. What point in this lesson had the most impact on you? Why?

2. When do you have the most difficulty controlling angry feelings? Which method in this lesson could help you in that situation?

3. Explain Proverbs 25:28 in relation to uncontrolled anger.

4. Paraphrase I Peter 2:19-23 in your own words. How could this focus help you control your anger.

2. Resentment & Bitterness

"A man's venom poisons himself more than his victim."

—Wings of Silver

THE PROBLEM

Have you ever been coldly indignant because you felt you were treated unfairly or insulted, your rights were violated, or someone had an unfair advantage? If so, you experienced resentment. Resentment is a painful emotion because it makes you feel cheated and mistreated, and it is a downhill road to self-pity, bitterness and hatred.

If you were unable to overcome your resentment, it more than likely developed into bitterness. Bitterness is a malignant form of resentment and it is capable of spreading rapidly to all areas of your life. It causes you to feel intense animosity, severe pain, grief and regret. It is harsh, reproachful and unpleasant. The Bible associates bitterness with misery.

Resentment Is Easily Justified

In many cases of resentment the *resentee* has truly been injured by the *resentor* and feels justified thinking, "What can you expect under the circumstances...you would be resentful too if..." Justifying sinful behaviors and attitudes due to circumstances has always

17

been one of Satan's most effective rationals. But for a Christian it is in direct opposition to the life he is committed to live, *"For it is commendable if a man bears up under the pain of unjust suffering because he is conscious of God."* (I Peter 2:19)

Resentment Is A Secondary Infection

Resentment can easily be compared to a secondary infection or complication of a physical condition. For example, pneumonia can develop from bronchitis, a lung condition, surgery, trauma, the common cold, or other physical disorders. In the same way resentment is usually a secondary infection of a spiritual disorder: unresolved anger, conflict over personal rights, selfishness, non-acceptance of God's provision, envy and jealousy. And though it must be treated swiftly and seriously lest it develop into bitterness and hatred, the best treatment is prevention.

Little mention is made of resentment in God's teachings, although He warns severely of the result and consequences of bitterness and hatred. Instead he focuses his instruction on the sources of these spiritual maladies.

The Most Common Forms of Resentment

Resentment can develop in any spiritual problem; however, there seem to be five major forms that afflict mankind:

The I'M MAD form. This type of resentment is very persistent and thrives in an atmosphere of unresolved anger. It is easily detected through its sullen appearance and basic cop outs, "It wouldn't do any good to talk about it, they won't listen...I shouldn't have to say anything, they know they owe me an apology...I can't get them to...They will never change..."

The IT'S NOT FAIR form. This is probably the most widely spread form of resentment. It develops rapidly where conflict over personal rights exists. It has an appealing persecution color and is usually accompanied by a popular theme, "It's not fair, I have rights too...It's not that I care for myself but they shouldn't be allowed to get away with that..."

The BIG I form. This chameleon-like form of resentment is often difficult to diagnose for it parades under many guises, but it is actually a secondary infection of selfishness. It is most easily detected by its *I/Me* focus, "Doesn't anyone care about what I want...When is it going to be my turn...I never get to do what I want..."

The I WISH form. This virilent type feeds on a primary infection of envy and jealousy and if left untreated literally makes life not worth living. It afflicts the mind with continual comparison, "Everything just falls into his lap while I have to work like a dog...I wish I had her looks and she had a wart on her nose...I resent the way she complains about how tough they have it; she doesn't know what tough is..."

The IF I COULD JUST form. It is easy to mistake angry frustration as the source of this form of resentment, when it actually develops from non-acceptance of God's provision. It has a frustrated or sorrowful dialogue of, "If I could just have...If I could just do...If I just wasn't..."

It's possible to recognize these symptoms in your life and be frustrated and overwhelmed because you do not know how to overcome them. But, acknowledging the truth opens the door to freedom.

THE SOLUTION

You always start with repentance. A repentant spirit that is resolved to be free of resentment and bitterness. Next, commit yourself to following God's way out of resentment, aware it will take effort and trust—effort to develop new attitudes and behaviors, and trust that God's methods work.

God's Remedies For Resentment

To treat resentment in our lives and ignore the underlying spiritual problem would be like diligently mopping up the leak from a broken water pipe and never mending the pipe. Therefore, it is necessary to honestly analyze your resentment and its point of origin. Then deal with the root problem (anger, envy, selfishness, etc.). Don't be surprised if you find more than one. Resentment is not the result of your circumstances. It results from your attitude about your circumstances. Therefore, the only safeguard for resentment is *Attitude Therapy*. When God's attitudes are patiently and consistently developed, they can help you resist painful attacks of resentment.

1. *The Total Heart Attitude.* Have you ever been pressured or forced to do something against your will, for example, clean a huge stack of dishes you did not dirty? And you were miserable with dread for an hour before and resentful and sullen during the hour of work. God's immunizing attitude for that type of resentment is called the Total Heart Attitude. It is based on Colossians 3:23, *"Whatever you do, work at it with all your heart, as working for the Lord, not for men."* Paul taught this to slaves who had no choice in what they did or for whom they did it. And he was able to promise them, *"The Lord will reward..."* in verse 24. There is joy in doing something willingly, well and with the right motive. In this attitude, the motive is you are working for the Lord, not men. The *willingly* makes it go quickly. The *well* makes it rewarding. When this attitude is part of your life, you will find you can be resentment free whether picking up dirty socks or mowing the lawn.

2. *Only the Truth Attitude.* Have you ever been suspected of something you didn't do, called a liar when you weren't, punished when you were innocent? God has a attitude to protect you from the resentment that often develops. It is called *Only the Truth* attitude, based on John 8:32, *"...know the truth and the truth will set you free."* Christ, by accepting only the truth, was free from inner

turmoil, conflict and resentment when he was accused of blasphemy, demon possession, etc. He dealt with false accusations in John 8:48-59 and 10:33-42 by answering them truthfully, doing his best to avoid persecution and then proceeding with his responsibilities. Christ refused to let unjust accusations claim his focus.

Proverbs 26:2, *"Like a fluttering sparrow or a darting swallow, an undeserved curse does not come to rest."* This teaches that an undeserved curse can do no permanent damage. It can and should be ignored, for it will not last—only the truth remains forever.

3. *The Follow Me Attitude.* Have you ever felt resentful because someone else was not doing what they should. God has a preventive attitude. It's called the *Follow Me* attitude based on John 21:22 ff. Jesus taught this attitude to Peter when he said to him concerning John, *"If I want him to remain alive until I return, what is that to you? You must follow me."* While Jesus was telling Peter what he would have him do, Peter looked around and asked the Lord what was to happen to John. Jesus told him pointedly it was none of his business, *"...what is it to you?"* He also told him pointedly what his business was—*"you must follow me."* Keeping your focus and attention on following Christ will protect you from painful bouts of resentment.

4. *The Thank God Attitude.* Have you ever felt resentful because the kids have the mumps, the car broke down, the washer overflowed, the telephone man didn't come and your husband is working late? God has a preventive attitude for you from I Thess. 5:18, *"...give thanks in all circumstances..."* For example, "Thank you God, that our children are recovering from this childhood disease; that I have a washer instead of washing in a stream as millions of others in the world; that I do not have to answer this phone all day; thank you for my husband that loves and cares for me, please bring him home safely." Paul said in Philippians 4:12, *"...I have learned the secret of being content in any and every situation."* Contentment and thankfulness are learned attitudes. Thank God you don't have to be born with them and that you can't learn them as Paul and others have.

21

5. *The What Next Attitude.* Have you ever felt resentful because it seems that things work out for everyone but you. God's safeguard is a What Next attitude based on Galatians 6:9-10, *"Let us not become weary in doing good...as we have opportunity, let us do good to all people..."* God teaches you to serve every time you have opportunity. One of the best defenses against resentment is a busy hand and a busy mind that has no idle hours to contemplate how others have it easier than you.

6. *The Giving Instead of Getting Attitude.* Have you ever felt resentful because someone took advantage of you? God has a preventive attitude for you. It is called a Giving Instead of Getting Attitude and is based on Matthew 5:38-48. In a condensed version that passage would read, "If someone strikes you—turn; if someone sues you—give; if someone forces you—go; if someone asks you— loan." Verse 45 explains why, *"that you may become sons of your Father in heaven."* This world dwells on what others owe you which makes you constantly aware of what you should be getting. God teaches you to focus on what you should be giving others regardless of what they do or do not give you.

Developing these attitudes and dealing with underlying spiritual problems will prevent and overcome a great deal of resentment and bitterness. But on occasions they are not potent enough to deal with the bitterness resulting from a deep personal injury.

Overcoming Bitterness

God's broad-spectrum antibiotic for bitterness is called *forgiveness.* It's easily available, but expensive and often difficult to administer. God, however, demands you use it, for he warns in Matthew 6:15, *"But if you do not forgive men their sins, your Father will not forgive your sins,"* Such strong motivation may make you sincerely want to forgive but your hurt is often so deep that you feel you just can't.

Understand What Forgiveness Is

To think you can't forgive is usually the result of not understanding forgiveness. Forgiveness is simply the way you behave toward the one who has hurt you. As a man, you want to base forgiveness on your *feelings*. You tend to think you must feel forgiving before you can forgive. But God knew the feelings would follow the action and he teaches you how to forgive by teaching you how to behave: (1) *"Do not repay evil with evil or insult with insult but with blessing...,"* I Peter 3:9 (2) *"If your enemy is hungry, give him food to eat, if he is thirsty, give him water to drink,"* Proverbs 25:21 (3) *"Bless those who persecute you...,"* Romans 12:14.

Notice in each passage that God is teaching you how to respond to someone that has hurt you or is hurting you. Christ taught this in the garden when he healed the ear of the soldier who came to take him to a false trial, Luke 22:51.

Get Out Of The Punishment Game

Forgiving a person is *returning blessing for cursing* and leaving the punishment in the hands of God. When you do not forgive you take their punishment into your hands, which can be a time consuming and painful process. Refusing to forgive is holding a grudge which is nothing more than *punishment on the installment plan.*

Develop A Forgiveness Focus

First, learn a lesson from Peter in Matthew 18 when he asked Jesus, *"Lord, how many times should I forgive someone, seven times?"* Peter might have been focusing on, *How much do I have to take?* Jesus gave him a somewhat unrealistic answer, *"seven times seventy."* He then went on to explain the principle in the parable of the Unmerciful Servant. He concluded in verse 32 and 33 when he taught that you can't afford to hold others' sins against them considering how many God could hold against you.

Secondly, practice focusing on your *response* instead of your *injury*. For example, if you discover a friend has made a vicious statement about you, instead of wallowing in pain wailing, "How can she do this to me after all I have done for her," focus on how God would have you react. Romans 12:17-21, *"Do not repay anyone evil for evil. Be careful to do what is right in the sight of everybody. If it is possible, as far as it depends on you, live at peace with everyone. Do not take revenge, my friends, but leave room for God's wrath, for it is written: 'It is mine to avenge, I will repay,' says the Lord.''* If your focus is on the wrong you have suffered you cannot help but become angry, resentful, unforgiving and bitter. *BUT,* if you focus on your response, follow through on what you know God teaches, you will come out with a forgiving heart and a clear conscience.

DISCUSSION QUESTIONS

1. What point in the lesson had the most impact on you? Why?

2. What type of resentment do you find the most difficult? Could a portion of this lesson help you in the future? Explain.

3. From Exodus 23:4-5 and Proverbs 25:21 is forgiveness a feeling or a behavior? Explain.

4. Name at least 3 benefits of forgiveness.

5. Can you forgive a person when they don't ask forgiveness? Proverbs 19:11: Ephesians 4:32.

3. Fear and Worry

"Worry is the most popular form of suicide."

—William George Jordan

THE PROBLEM

Along the highways of the Southwest are road signs reading, "Do not drive into blowing dust." On clear sunny days these signs seem ridiculous to the newcomer. But in a matter of minutes the sun can become obscured, the highway disappear from sight, and the lovely mountains seem to vanish. One feels lost, isolated, trapped and panicky. It is a strange hostile world.

Fear and worry have the same effect. Your life can be full and joyful until the blowing dust of fear and worry surround you. Then you lose your sense of perspective. The landmarks of God's care and protection are obscured. You feel forsaken and bewildered. You cannot see beyond the present storm.

These are powerful tools of Satan. With fear he can control you. When you are afraid, you are open to negative suggestions. "It won't work...you can't do anything about it...you'll not be accepted...it will hurt..." If you fall into the habit of listening to these thoughts, Satan can feed you endless discouraging ideas. He knows that you cannot be productive when you are fearful. Fear can claim all of your mind.

Worry is similar but it claims only part of your mind. With worry (fretting, anxiety) you have a divided mind. You are not able to be whole-hearted about anything. Worry eats away little by little like a cancer. "What if...maybe...how can I..." are worry words. As a Christian you do not finger worry beads, but you may be repeating worry words. Worry is a very real expression of lack of faith. God has promised his care for you, but you are saying, when you worry, "I am not sure I can trust you."

Fear and worry are different, but the results of each are the same. The process of overcoming them is the same. Therefore, they are covered together in this chapter.

Bible Acknowledgement of Fear and Worry

The twenty-third Psalm is probably the best loved portion of the Bible. It speaks of the areas that worry mankind: food and drink, a place to rest, direction, illness, death and evil. It then asserts that God (the shepherd) will care for you (the sheep) in those situations. *"He makes me...he leads me...he guides me...you are with me...you prepare...you annoint."* The conclusion is *"Surely goodness and love will follow me all the days of my life, and I will dwell in the house of the Lord forever."*

Jesus taught directly about fear. In the parable of the talents (Matthew 25:14-30), the one-talent man was unprofitable because he was afraid. *"So I was afraid, and went out and hid your talent in the ground."* He was condemned severely for this attitude.

One night Jesus approached the apostles by walking across the sea. (Matthew 14:22-33) As he came in sight they were terrified, but he reassured them saying, *"Take courage! It is I. Don't be afraid."* With that in his mind, Peter set out across the water also to meet Jesus, but soon he was overcome by fear again. *"But when he saw the wind, he was afraid..."* Fears are not easily overcome. They reappear unexpectedly and often. Just when you may feel they are behind you, a situation arises that triggers the *fear* response again.

Martha's rebuke from Jesus came not because she was caring for physical needs, but because she was fretting about her work. *"Martha, Martha,...you are worried and upset about many things."*

(Luke 10:41) Fretfulness is another expression of worry. Anxiety and a troubled spirit hinder effectiveness. Whether you are involved in homemaking as Martha was; teaching; working in an office; selling; or whatever, allowing yourself to become upset and worried is harmful not only to you, but to your work. You cannot be efficient and productive with the divided mind that comes when worries stake a claim in your thinking.

"What If..."

"What if" is a favorite game of worriers.
What if........

> it rains
> I'm late
> I become ill
> there is not enough money
> this is the wrong decision
> my child takes drugs
> my child gets hurt
> I'm left all alone
> my mate stops loving me
> I make them angry
> there was an accident
> I have to move
> I lose my job

So much worry is based on possibilities for the future—borrowing trouble from tomorrow. This is wasteful in terms of time, energy, and accomplishments for today. *"Therefore do not worry about tomorrow, for tomorrow will worry about itself. Each day has enough trouble of its own."* (Matthew 6:34).

What Fear and Worry Do

Earlier in Matthew 6 Jesus speaks specifically of worry and condemns this attitude as a lack of faith (25-33). *"Therefore I tell you, do not worry about your life...Oh you of little faith."* Worry is sinful and *separates* you from God. Therefore, you must develop the ability to overcome worry.

Fear paralyzes you until you are not capable of constructive action. Soon after I was married, one evening I noticed an unusual light shining through the curtains of our house. I thought someone was prowling around trying to get in. It frightened me so much that I could not even speak to tell my husband who was only a few feet away. Eventually I realized the light was only a reflection from a mirror lying in my own lap. Many of our terrified moments come from such a silly misunderstanding. How foolish to let any outside influence, whether real or imagined, incapacitate us from action.

Another result of fear and worry is that *they are contagious.* Children have the uncanny ability to sense any fear or concern in their parents and immediately assimilate that into their own thinking. A young family moved to an area where tornadoes are prevalent. The children's experiences with storms had been limited to mild thunder and lightning so they were not afraid. Soon after the move a tornado struck their new town and the mother was terrified even though she was not in the path of destruction. The next morning she took the children to view the damage. They saw her fear and the reason for it. Because of their limited understanding, they could not handle their fears and became hysterical when it thundered after that incident. Even adults 'catch' fear or uneasiness from others. With a visible disease, care is taken to keep from spreading it. The same care needs to be used in regard to fear and worry. You need to ask yourself, "Am I a carrier of fear disease? Am I an infectious center for worry?"

THE SOLUTION

People try to overcome fear and worry but are not successful, so they conclude they can never be victorious in this area. This conclusion is not in accord with biblical promises. *"For God did not give us a spirit of timidity (fear) but a spirit of power, of love and of self-discipline."* (2 Timothy 1:7) You can use the tools given you by God to conquer fear which is NOT from God.

He has given **power**—an unlimited power. How foolish to be afraid when you have more power than the cause of your fear. A young child may fear the neighborhood bully, but his father can laugh at the threats because the adult is bigger and more powerful. As Christians "grow up" the fears diminish.

He has given **love**. This love not only extends *to* you, but continues on *through* you to others. You do not have to manufacture love, only nurture it as it passes through you. It is difficult to fear that which you love. *"There is no fear in love. But perfect love drives out fear..."* (I John 4:18).

He has given **self-discipline**. Sometimes the only way to overcome fear is to give yourself a mental shake and determine to drive it out. Loose dried grass clinging to clothing can be picked off piece by piece, but a quicker more effective way is to shake the garment. Tackling your fears and worries one by one can be an endless discouraging process, but disciplining yourself in the overall rejection of fear and worry hits at the basis of the sin.

The spirit of fear which is *not* from God cannot co-exist with the spirit of power, of love, and of self-discipline which *is* from God.

Facing Fears

It has been said that the best cattle to have in a snow storm are Hereford. Other breeds drift as the wind and snow assail them until they come against an obstacle such as a fence or building; then, when they can drift no further, the snow covers them and they freeze. A Hereford herd will face the storm, standing their ground. The snow blows past them and does not drift over them since there is no barrier. Thus, they are able to survive the storm. Only by facing fears and worries head-on can progress in conquering them be made. Trying to avoid the situations or people who cause worries only intensifies them; it will not help in overcoming them.

Four Steps

Here are four steps to conquering fear and worry in your life:

1. *Identify the worries and fears.* List each one, whether real or only a possibility, whether major or minor. Your list might include such things as a health problem, loss of someone close to you, a dentist's drill, your appearance, financial struggles, storms, your l6-year old soloing in the family car, airplanes, mountain roads, being alone at night, etc.

Now decide which are **real.** Sometimes an honest look at the validity of a worry or fear can reduce it. If the moisture from a 100-foot high cloud covering seven city blocks were condensed, it would fill only one average-sized glass. Worries need to be condensed to a size that can be handled. Montaigne, a French philosopher, said, "My life has been full of terrible misfortunes, most of which never happened."

2. *Recall the times God has rescued you.* It is so good to keep a prayer list, then record on it each time God answered a specific prayer. This builds trust in his love and care.

Most worries are recurring. If you had listed worries last year (or even five years ago) then compared them to today's list, you would find many of the same items. When a worry recurs remember that God led you through that situation before and will do it again.

3. *Pray.* God has promised strength and comfort when you ask. *"Cast all your anxiety on him because he cares for you."* (I Peter 5:7). When you turn to him, he provides a peace beyond explanation. *"Do not be anxious about anything, but in everything by prayer and petition with thanksgiving present your requests to God. And the peace of God which transcends all understanding will guard your hearts and your minds in Christ Jesus."* (Philippians 4:6-7). Use the list of fears and worries you made and talk with God about them one by one. There is nothing on your list that is not covered by the phrase *"do not be anxious about anything."* When you do this, he has promised to *"keep your heart and your mind."* Let him control your heart and your mind.

Jesus in the garden before his death knew anxiety, even fear. He used the avenue of prayer to be able to face the fearful times ahead. He allowed God to control his mind, and thus his actions.

4. *Trust in God's promises to care for you.* In his last speech Joshua reminded the Israelites of God's dependability: *"...that not one of all the good promises has been fulfilled, not one has failed."* (Joshua 23:14) You can depend on God to keep his promises concerning your care.

The following verses need to be read often—even memorized—to comfort and to encourage you in your trust of the Lord. They can be named "trust-building" scriptures.

Philippians 4:4-8	Hebrews 13:6
Proverbs 3:24	Psalms 37:25
Matthew 28:20	Mark 5:36
Romans 8:28,37-39	1 John 4:18

DISCUSSION QUESTIONS

1. List the things you fear and/or worry about. Be specific. Which are "real"?

2. Relate a time God has rescued you when you saw no solution.

3. What is God's prescription for worry and fear? 1 Peter 5:7; Philippians 4:6-7; Mark 5:36; Matthew 6:25-34; 1 John 4:18.

4. Discuss the *trust-building* scriptures.

4. Depression

"Weeping endureth for the night but joy cometh in the morning."

—Psalms 30:5

THE PROBLEM

Jane was lying on the couch staring at a TV game show. The breakfast dishes were on the table, she was in her housecoat, her husband would be home in a couple of hours. Her eyes filled with tears as she anticipated how disgusted and angry he would be with the mess. Jane was suffering from depression.

The depth of depression can vary from a prolonged case of the blahs to very serious mental, emotional, and physical illness. Its symptoms are many and experienced in a variety of combinations: eating problems, erratic sleep patterns, unkempt appearance, neglected chores, loss of affection, indifference, sadness (weeps), irritability, hostility, anxiety, fear, worry, hopelessness and numerous physical ailments.

In the United States each year there are from 50,000 to 70,000 suicides and over half of these are attributed to depression. Annually, 125,000 are hospitalized and treated for depression and another 200,000 are treated privately. Yet, there are many times that number who suffer from depression and are never treated professionally.

It is not just a contemporary problem. Hippocrates wrote on the subject in the 4th century B.C. and named it *melancholia,* meaning heavy, dark red blood, which he thought was responsible for the symptoms. (And if you have ever been depressed you can understand part of his reasoning.)

It has been widely studied for years; thus reams of material have been published on the subject, yet it remains as much a problem today as ever.

What Causes Depression

Science does not have an answer to this question. Scientists have developed a variety of methods to treat the symptoms of depression but the cause eludes them. They have vast amounts of information concerning depression and have discovered: (1) it is a universal problem, (2) all age groups are susceptible, (3) some people are more prone to depression than others, (4) the degree of depression varies, (5) no group or individual is totally immune, and (6) depression always starts with an external event. All of these observations coincide with the Biblical insight on depression but the last is by far the most significant.

Depression always starts with an event. Consider how many times you hear, "I am so depressed over this, or over that, or over something else." Such statements indicate the external event of their depression. However, it is possible to be depressed and be totally unaware of the event triggering it, but you can be confident there is one.

How Does Depression Develop

Depression can develop slowly or instantly. However, it usually starts with a feeling of the blahs and a few days of "I don't want to do anything today." If unchecked it progresses into fatigue, irritability, eating problems, and tears as things begin to stack up. Or occasionally an event will be so traumatic that you go instantly into the depths of full-blown depression characteristic by uncontrolled weeping, nausea, and feelings of hopelessness, etc.

Man can do about the same thing for depression that he can for the common cold—treat the symptoms, which is not to be taken lightly. For although, it may not cure the depression, it often makes the depressed more comfortable and can be of help while one is seeking the solution.

THE SOLUTION

God's solution to depression is based on "response." He teaches you to respond to "external events" in a manner that avoids depression. Man has discovered that depression always starts with an external event; and God's teachings (Genesis 4:5-7) indicate that the way you respond to an event can either lift your countenance up or let your countenance fall (depression).

To better understand this concept, let's use a mental visual aid. Imagine a beautiful country road running along the upper edge of a valley. Along this road are several exits that lead south toward the valley. All of these exits have a junction where you can either turn north back to the upper valley road or continue on down to the heart of the valley. Now, let the upper valley road represent the life's journey God would have you travel; the exits represent events that can or will occur in your life; the road continuing down into the valley are Roads of Depression; and the valley shall be the Valley of Despair. With this mental image let's study God's solution to depression.

Exit of Disappointment

Everyone that lives travels many side roads of disappointment. Some are large, some small; but all are capable of detouring you onto the Road of Depression if not handled God's way.

Disappointments arise from many different sources: job situations, longed-for goals, financial desires, and the most common of all, people (wives, husbands, children, Christians, friends, etc.). A disapppointment is really nothing more than an unfulfilled expectation and all such side roads should be required to have a sign posted that reads, "Watch Out For Falling Expectations."

Consider the things you become disappointed and depressed over which are nothing more than expectations that did not come true: the house you wanted but someone else got, the promotion you worked for and an outside man received, the son that joined the Marines instead of finishing school, or the party you prepared for 30 and 6 showed up. All of these were *wants* and *dreams* that did not come true for whatever the reason.

When your dreams shatter you often turn aside into the lane of disappointment. This lane quickly approaches a junction where you may choose to turn back north to the upper valley road or south on the Road of Depression to the Valley of Despair.

Few people want to be on the Road of Depression, for it's well known as a bad trip, but many travel it anyway, unaware they have a choice. It has a comforting sign that reads, "What can you expect? Who wouldn't be depressed?" which offers momentary relief. While the road north to the upper valley is obviously a toll road, and feeling bankrupt from disappointment, it is just easier to turn south to depression. But if you investigate a little more closely you will notice a sign along the northbound road which reads, "This road provided by the courtesy of God. Free tokens available in Scripture for toll fees."

For the return from the Lane of Disappointment two tokens have been provided: The Token of Blessing and The Token of Purpose.

The Token of Blessing. Paul used this token a great deal during his life and it protected him from the road of depression. One example is 2 Timothy 1:15-18. In verse 15 Paul states, *"You know that every one in the province of Asia has deserted me..."* (a disappointment no doubt) and then he devotes verses 16-17 to expressing his gratitude to Onesiphous who had helped him so much. From this passage we can see that Paul acknowledged a disappointing fact that concerned *"everyone in the province of Asia"* but focused his attention on the blessing one man was to him.

The Token of Purpose. In 2 Timothy 2:9-10, Paul used a second token for dealing with disappointment. In this passage he tells Timothy that his imprisonment (a disappointment) is the result of his preaching Christ. Then he points out, *"...I endure everything for the sake of the elect, that they may obtain the salvation that is in Christ Jesus...."* His words emphasize the fact he never lost sight of the purpose of his life—reconciling man to God (2 Corinthians 5:19).

By using these two tokens, i.e., focusing on his blessings and remembering his life purpose, Paul could return to the upper valley road when caught on a lane of disappointment without travelling the Road of Depression and the Valley of Despair.

What of the Road to Depression?

The Road of Depression is paved with components of anger and self-pity, sometimes visible, sometimes concealed but nevertheless there. For they are the responses to external events (disappointment, rejection, illness, comparison, ambivalence, etc.) that trigger depression. The proportion of self-pity to anger determines how rapidly and to what depth you descend into the Valley of Despair.

Paul could have chosen this road in either situation and made it sound quite justifiable. For example, he could have said, "I risked my life to teach the people of Asia, gave so much of myself for them and now everyone of them has deserted me but one. Some thanks." Or he might have thought, "I don't understand, I have worked as hard as I can for God, given up everything for Him—family, friends, prestige, wealth, etc., and He lets me rot in this prison when all I was doing was trying to serve Him." Had Paul chosen to respond in this way he would have found himself catapulting full speed into depression.

The Exit of Comparison

The Exit of Comparison is a quick trip on the Road of Depression. And if it doesn't lead to depression it usually leads to sin. Consider, if you compare yourself or situation to someone that appears to have less going for them, pride and smugness will likely be the outcome. If you compare yourself to someone that appears to have it better than you, discouragement, envy, jealousy, and a poor self-image will possibly be the result. Either way you lose.

However, it is the second situation of comparison that detours many into depression. It's easy to become depressed when you: (1) look at people who never seem to have a problem of any kind while your life is just one crisis after another, or (2) see how well-behaved and loving your neighbor's children are when yours act like they hate you, or (3) watch your slender sister gourge herself and not gain a pound while you have starved all of your chubby life, or (4) notice the way your friend's husband appreciates her when she doesn't even try to be a good wife.

For the frustrating Exit of Comparison God has provided the Token of Imitation to return you to the depression-free upper valley.

The Token of Imitation. Scripture never encourages us to compare ourselves to others. Instead it commands us to imitate God and Christ (Matthew 5:48; Luke 6:36; John 13:15; I John 2:6). *"To this you were called, because Christ suffered for you leaving you an example, that you should follow in his steps."* (I Peter 2:21). To follow anyone's example is an admission they are preceeding you in the direction you want to go. And that admission protects you from pride and the concentration it takes to follow protects you from the discouragement of comparison. Paul encourages us to follow the example of himself and others that are following Christ. *"Join with others in following my example, brothers, and take note of those who live according to the pattern we gave you."* (Philippians 3:17). All of these scriptures focus on imitation of Christ and faithful Christians instead of "comparison."

The Exit of Illness

Short sideroads of illness that we all must take occasionally, rarely lead to serious depression. But prolonged periods on these detours of illness make you particularly vulnerable to depression.

The sideroad of prolonged or chronic illness is probably the most dangerous of all. It is paved with continuous frustration. It is flooded by frequent storms of guilt because your family and friends are being forced to ride along carrying much of the load of your illness. It is usually travelled DWI (Driving While under the Influence of drugs and medication) affecting your emotional and mental attitude. And it seems the road is on an incline, which means if you relax your grip for a moment you automatically angle into the valley of despair.

As you consider the obstacles of this road you are almost overwhelmed until you remember that when you are weakest in yourself, Christ is the strongest in you. Only in your weakness is God made perfect (2 Corinthians 12:9,10). When once you grasp the impact of this passage you will discover God can take your lane of illness and transform it into the upper valley road!

For this lane you have been given the most powerful tokens of all—the Token of Glory and the Token of Concern for Others (a pain medication).

The Token of Glory. John in chapter nine tells of a man that had been given this token. Jesus healed him after he had been blind for 40 years, and said his blindness was, *"so the work of God could be displayed in his life."* The healing took minutes but the man had lived in blindness toward this moment for 40 years. Through Christ's touch he was given physical sight that glorified God, and through his response to Christ he was given spiritual sight which was even a greater glory to God. Every time you respond God's way while on this road the token of glory is magnified in your life. In the same way Christ's greatest glory for God was during his greatest humiliation and physical pain on the cross.

The Token of Concern for Others. Christ used this token on the cross. Of the seven statements made during this agony, four expressed concern for other people. Only this focus away from self can ease the pain on the Exit of Illness.

The Exit of Rejection

All of us will at some time be forced into a lane of rejection. It may be as simple as the family dog not liking you; or as painful as

39

your 13-year old daughter wishing your best friend was her mother; or as shattering as your husband of 17 years wanting a divorce to marry a 22-year old file clerk. Whatever the situation, the lane of rejection is never easy. It is painful by itself but it usually merges with the lane of disappointment, and the two form a rut that appears impossible to cross, avoid, or escape.

But you can be confident that God never allows you to be burdened with anything he doesn't give you the strength to bear or avoid. The road of rejection is no exception. To return to the upper valley, God has provided three tokens: the Token of Acceptance, the Token of Purpose and the Token of Forgiveness.

The Token of Acceptance. Rejection often is an unpleasant side effect of God's gift to man—the power of choice. Your life becomes unbearably frustrating when you refuse to accept the choice of a rejector. Christ was wounded by rejection and remained open to reconciliation (through forgiveness) but he always accepted the rejector's decision. And until you are willing to use this token you cannot escape the road of rejection, instead you will just travel it over and over again.

The Token of Purpose. Jesus was often rejected but was never "bogged down" because he had his purpose firmly in mind. And it was following this purpose that protected him in John 7:2-14. There his own brothers did not believe and were apparently embarrassed by his behavior. Christ responded by accepting their decision then going about fulfilling his purpose. In dealing with rejection he consistently followed 3 steps: (1) he taught and loved a would-be rejector as he did everyone else, (2) he accepted their decision, and (3) he continued with his Father's business regardless of the path they chose. Paul teaches this same principle in 1 Corinthians 7:12-15 concerning a believer's response to an unbelieving mate's desire to dissolve the marriage.

The Token of Forgiveness. You cannot overcome rejection until you forgive your rejector, as Jesus did on the cross when he prayed, *"forgive them..."* (Luke 23:34). Jesus was aware his rejectors did not totally understand and consequently did not appreciate what he was offering them, but he recognized their decision was their responsibility as forgiveness was his. Therefore, he did not respond with fury, revenge, and contempt. Instead he responded with sorrow and forgiveness as taught in Romans 12:17-21.

The Exit of Ambivalence

The lane of ambivalence is one of the most miserable of all sideroads. It is permeated by a sense of being trapped with no possible way out. The hopeless, trapped feelings of ambivalence can arise from many sources, i.e., marital problems, financial burdens, frustrating job situations, unfulfilled expectations, health problems, too many unrelieved days in the house, etc.

These feelings often result from: (1) decisions you would like to back out of instead of work through, or (2) circumstances in which you have no choice. The first category would consist of such things as unwise spending that has created serious financial problems or the dream marriage that is gradually turning into a nightmare. The second category (where you have no choice) might be: three months of strep throat, tonsillitis and ear infections with three "below-school-age" children or your husband losing his job two months before the new baby is due.

But take heart, God will not allow you to be caught in a trap that is eternal or hopeless. You can return to the upper valley with The Token of Straight Ahead, The Token of Promise, and The Token of Humility.

The Token of Straight Ahead. There is only one way out of ambivalent feelings—straight ahead. We often try to remake the decisions that got us there, but you can only repent of past decisions not re-decide them. Decisions are made for the future or straight ahead. Even if you are on this lane through no decision of your own the only way off is work (or live) through it. This token is called "perseverance" in scripture and is a characteristic of the mature Christian life (James 1:2-4).

The Token of Promise. God promises that trials (which an ambivalent situation certainly is) produces perseverance, and perseverance is the only way out of a trial. So no ambivalent lane is eternal or hopeless, for the longer you stay there, the greater perseverance you develop and with greater perseverance comes greater ability to return to the upper valley (Romans 5:3-5).

The Token of Humility. You are sometimes trapped in ambivalent situations because you haven't thought "straight ahead" and made the necessary decisions. But other times you honestly don't know how to get out; in that case—**ASK.** (Romans 15:14). All it will cost is a little pride, and God has provided this token for that situation.

We Could Go On and On

We could continue to find situations that are capable of triggering depression for the next 20 pages. But no doubt you understand the basis now for overcoming depression that is not physically induced. Depression does not result from your situation or circumstances but from our response or attitude regarding that situation or circumstances.

I Am Living Proof

The first time I was confronted with this concept I became very indignant, for I was struggling with a fairly serious depression. I was recovering from a long period of illness, feeling guilty about the heavy emotional, physical, and financial burdens my illness had created for my family, suffering frustration with a teenage daughter who was suddenly skipping school, and resenting the things my physical condition would not allow me to do. As I lay on the couch exhausted and frustrated, I honestly and objectively listened to my thinking patterns for the first time since my depression began, "It's not fair...we have tried so hard...the bills..." It was true, I was angry about the situation and wallowing in self-pity.

Thank God I understood his principles enough to realize I had to deal with my anger and self-pity if I ever intended to live a useful, happy life again. For as long as I justified my depression I would not be able to overcome it. I would have to trust God when he said in I Corinthians 10:12-13 that he would not allow me to have more than I could bear (although in this situation I was convinced he was overestimating me).

However, once I got up, quit feeling sorry for myself and started dealing (living through) my problems, relying on God, my depression disappeared. It took longer to get through the problems—but eventually even they disappeared. Now I thank God for the blessing I received from those problems, for the language of pain and compassion they taught me, and most of all for the meaning they gave to Psalms 30:5, *"Weeping endureth for the night. But joy cometh in the morning."*

DISCUSSION QUESTIONS

1. What point in this lesson had the most impact on you? Why?

2. When are you the most tempted to become depressed?

3. How does depression interfere with your Christian life?

4. How can a lack of goals or purpose lead to depression?

5. What triggered Cain's anger and depression in Genesis 4:1-7?

For an in depth study of depression from a Christian perspective, the reader is referred to an excellent book *Happiness Is A Choice*(Baker Book House) by Psychiatrists Meir and Minrith. (Although, the author does not share or recommend all of his Theological positions.)

5. Pri-I-de

"True humility is intelligent self-respect which keeps us from thinking too highly or too meanly of ourselves. It makes us mindful of the nobility God meant us to have, yet it makes us modest by reminding us how far we come short of what we can be."

—Ralph Sockman

THE PROBLEM

Luke 18:9-14 gives a clear picture of pride in action. In modern times it might read like this:

> To some who were confident of their own righteousness and looked down on everybody else, Jesus told this parable: Two women went to worship on Sunday morning. One was a Bible class teacher and the other was a new Christian with many problems. The teacher sang heartily, looking around her as she thought to herself, "God, I thank you that I am not like others, cheating in business, letting my children run wild, drinking, partying, or even like this new Christian. I teach Bible class, I never miss a service, I contribute liberally." But the new Christian sang softly, meditating on her words with her eyes lowered and prayed as she sang, "God, have mercy on me, a sinner." I tell you the last woman left the worship justified rather than the first; for everyone who exalts himself will be humbled, but he who humbles himself will be exalted.

Identifying Pride

It is easy to identify pride in others (by their speech, their body movements, their interactions with people), but it is *not* easy to recognize pride in one's own life.

45

One of my family's favorite recreations is hiking on back-country trails. As we walk along, I often warn my children of roots or rocks in the path that could trip them. One day my daughter was particularly careless and had fallen several times. I admonished her, "Be sure-footed." Just as I said the words, I slipped on loose sand and skinned my leg. She immediately began comforting me, then said, "Mommy, you forgot to be sure-footed." I was so concerned with the dangers to her that I took my eyes off my own steps.

This is what Christians do with pride. While you are warning others of sins that may cause them to fall, you may slide on the loose sands of pride. You are not being sure-footed. Because pride is not an outward obvious sin, but a subtle inner sin, you may not see it until you have skinned or bruised your spiritual body.

Satan spreads the loose sand of pride liberally. God warns us often throughout the scriptures to be sure-footed. *"Pride goes before destruction, a haughty spirit before a fall."* (Proverbs 16:18) He is telling you to watch for the sands of pride so that you will not fall on them and be destroyed.

Camouflaged Pride

One way Satan camouflages pride is by using it as a synonym for self-respect. When pride is discussed in the Bible, it is a negative trait, not a positive self-respect. *"We have heard of Moab's pride—her overwhelming pride and conceit, her pride and her insolence..."* (Isaiah 16:6). This description does not sound like something to be desired as self-respect is.

True synonyms for pride are vanity, arrogance, haughtiness and disdain. When the word "pride" is used, substitute one of these synonyms; then it is easier to recognize the sin.

How Pride Acts

Pride (disdain) will cause sin in so many related ways—jealousy, gossip, harshness, criticism, rebellion, ingratitude, lying, and anger are just a few that are often symptoms of the deeper sin of pride (disdain).

Pride (haughtiness) will cause you to measure others by yourself and yourself by others. As long as you can place yourself above at least one other person, then you feel confident and satisfied. This is not the measuring standard found in the Bible. *"Be perfect, therefore, as your heavenly Father is perfect."* (Matthew 5:48) *"Follow my example, as I follow the example of Christ."* (I Corinthians 11:1) Christ is the only accurate way to measure your development as a Christian. Since each one fails in some way to meet the perfect standard, there is no room left for pride (haughtiness).

Saving face is really a cover up for pride (vanity). For example, you may excuse your poor behavior on the basis of circumstances, or you may not be able to apologize or admit wrongdoing, or you could hide your inadequacies by calling attention to your own strong points and the weakness of others. All of this is done because pride (vanity) will not allow honesty in looking at yourself.

Pride (arrogance) will make you believe you are the only one who can do a job. When you are not able to allow another freedom in carrying out an assignment because you are afraid he will muff the job, you need to check your pride (arrogance). Many Christians have been discouraged from growing in areas of service to Christ because some one was too proud of his own abilities to permit a faltering attempt to be made by a novice.

Kinds of Pride

Although pride is present in every area of life, the scriptures seem to discuss four places where pride will likely cause a Christian to slip.

The Sands of Spiritual Pride (Haughtiness)

This is the pride described in the parable of the Pharisee and the publican rewritten at the beginning of this lesson. It is also found in the teachers and the Pharisees when they brought the adulterous woman to Jesus (John 8:3-11). It is often linked to the Pharisees in

47

Jesus' teachings. Because their whole life was centered around minute law-keeping, it was easy for them to fall into this sin.

They became so enraptured with their own righteousness in the details of their lives that they completely blotted out the sins of attitude and were able to delude themselves into believing in their own goodness. They were also proud of their religious position and the resulting prestige.

This is hateful to God and will be punished severely. Mark 12:38-40 shows God's feelings about spiritual pride. *"As he taught, Jesus said, 'Watch out for the teachers of the law. They like to walk around in flowing robes and be greeted in the marketplaces, and have the most important seats in the synagogues and places of honor at banquets. They devour widows' houses and for a show make lengthy prayers. Such men will be punished most severely.' "*

It is important that religiously active people today guard against slipping on the same sands. When one has invested hours in study, effort in serving, and money in helping others, it is a great temptation to be self-congratulatory and superior. It is also easy to become proud of the role of service one has been assigned. Bible class teaching, supervising other teachers, committee leadership, etc., can all be a source of pride.

The Sands of Intellectual Pride (Arrogance)

How many times have highly educated men and women drifted far from God and His Word as the result of depending on their own knowledge and reason. It is never safe to build a philosophy on one's own wisdom. *"Do you see a man wise in his own eyes? There is more hope for a fool than for him."* (Proverbs 26:12) Only through the seemingly simple, even foolish, faith in the word of God can true wisdom be found. *"For the message of the cross is foolishness to those who are perishing, but to us who are being saved it is the power of God."* (I Corinthians 1:18) The value of a person is not measured by the score on a I.Q. test or the list of earned degrees.

But in contrast, there are those who pride themselves on lack of education or training. This is only another form of the same snobbery. A self-made man can never rise above himself. The answer is not to take pride in your own ability in overcoming a lack of education, but to allow God to use what you are. He can make you rise to unimagined heights.

Jesus called the educated and the uneducated to work together and to follow him. Even among his closest followers were uneducated fishermen and highly trained teachers and doctors.

The Sands of Material Pride (Vanity)

Over and over God warns that the rich will fight great temptations, particularly in regard to pride. *"People who want to get rich fall into temptation and a trap and into many foolish and harmful desires that plunge men into ruin and destruction."* (I Timothy 6:9) He tells you to remember that the ability to gain wealth came from him. *"You may say to yourself, 'My power and the strength of my hands have produced this wealth for me.' But remember the Lord your God, for it is he who gives you the ability to produce wealth, and so confirms his covenant, which he swore to your forefathers, as it is today."* (Deuteronomy 8:17,18) It is easy to let possessions possess you, to let them become the focal point of your life, rather than relegating them to the role of an aid in serving God.

As with intellectual pride, a reverse pride can be present in regard to material wealth. There are those who are proud of poverty and even those who feign poverty who in reality have an abundance, thinking poverty is equal to spirituality.

> "Some people are proud of wearing new clothes and driving new cars. Not I! I'm proud of wearing old clothes and driving old cars. Which only proves that I think my pride is better than yours—in my humble opinion." Norman Gipson

There is no special merit in not having wealth, just as there is no honor in Christ in being wealthy. The humility of accepting what you have gratefully and realizing who provides it is the proper attitude.

The Sands of Social Pride (Disdain)

James discusses this problem in chapter two. *"My brothers, as believers in our glorious Lord Jesus Christ, don't show favoritism... If you show special attention to the man wearing fine clothes...have you not discriminated among yourselves and become judges with evil thoughts?"* Even the mother of James and John was guilty of wanting social prominence for her sons. (Matthew 20:20-28)

The early church had a distinct problem with emphasis on social standing, and along with this emphasis developed a pride in one's social status. It is easy to see how this could happen in the context of the general society of that day. All of life was governed by one's social standing.

Today there is more sophistication in outlook, and social barriers are blurred, yet there remains a remnant of pride. Rather than being based on where in the strata one was born, it is based on how high one has climbed. Movie and TV stars, sports heros, social leaders, etc., are given special honor based not on their contributions to mankind or their piety, but rather on their claim to fame.

Some pride often causes one to withdraw inwardly from people who are boorish, ill-mannered, immature, unkempt, or troubled, and even from those considered to be above him in some way, such as bosses, those in the social register, community leaders, etc. The gospel was extended to all equally, and Jesus responded to all who came to him. He answered to beggars and the military leaders, the prostitutes and the religious counselors. His followers can do no less.

Seriousness of Pride

The Old Testament abounds with warnings against pride. *"The Lord detests all the proud of heart. Be sure of this: They will not go unpunished."* (Proverbs 16:5; See also Psalms 101:5; Proverbs 16:18,19; Isaiah 2:11,12.)

King Nebuchadnezzar experienced the wrath of God against pride when he praised himself for his vast kingdom. The Lord caused him to lose his reason, to lose his kingdom, and to live literally as an animal. When his reason returned and he praised God rather than himself, his kingdom was restored. His comment was, *"Now, I, Nebuchadnezzar, praise and exalt and glorify the King of heaven, because everything he does is right and all his ways are just. And those who walk in pride he is able to humble."* (Daniel 4:28-37)

Herod, of the New Testament, also experienced God's immediate retaliation against pride when he was infested with worms and died. (Acts 12:21-24) Other warnings can be found in Romans 12:3; Galatians 6:3; 1 Peter 5:5; and 1 John 2:16,17. It seems as if God cannot emphasize too much how he opposes the proud.

THE SOLUTION

Pride can be conquered. *"I can do everything through him who gives me strength."* (Philippians 4:13) When Jesus was teaching the rich young ruler about pride in his material possessions, the apostles took note that the young man was not ready to give this up. Jesus told them it would be hard to conquer this pride. *"When the disciples heard this, they were greatly astonished and asked, 'Who then can be saved?'"* (Matthew 19:25) But Jesus reassured them that it was possible. *"Jesus looked at them and said, 'With man this is impossible, but with God all things are possible.'"* (verse 26) The solution begins with asking for God's help in seeing and avoiding the sands of pride.

It takes continuous watching along the path. When walking past one section of loose dirt successfully, one does not decide that now he is safe for the rest of the hike. Again and again he will pass areas of danger. Just as you have conquered pride in one area, it appears in your life in another place. It can even be pride at having overcome pride! There is a story about a man who was awarded a button saying, "The Most Humble Man of the Year." It was taken away from him when he wore it because he was proud of being humble.

There are some steps you can take to avoid pride in your life.

1. One way to lessen the danger of slipping on pride is to *acknowledge your own sinfulness.* When you see anger, gossip, envy, lust, or other sins in your life and face them, there is not a feeling of pride left, only one of humility and gratitude for God's forgiveness.

2. Another way is to recognize that all you have or can do *comes from God.* His gifts to you are abundant and you can see the worth he places on you in bestowing them, but you must remember their source. Along with this remembrance needs to be a prayer that what you have or can do be used for God's glory and not for self-glory.

3. Seeing and praising the *gifts* God has *bestowed on another* will also smother pride. When you can deliberately turn attention away from your own accomplishments to those of someone else, you have made a great gain on pride. This is an exercise that can be practiced, and with practice becomes a way of life.

4. The final way to rid a life of pride is to *die to self.* "I" is the center of pr-I-de both in spelling and in living. As long as a person is thinking of HIMself, HIS needs, HIS deeds, and HIS role, he will be full of pride. However, when he can forget himself and concentrate on the other person, pride will dissolve.

Warning

As stated earlier, pride and self-respect are not synonymous. While pride must be eliminated from your life, self-respect is essential. You are a person of worth in God's sight. You are the highest of his creation. You are the object of his love in sending his son for your salvation. Therefore, you must recognize your worth. False humility is not an antidote for pride. In fact, it is another form of pride. By depreciating yourself, you are belittling God's handiwork. Only by recognizing this worth can you be of use to God.

DISCUSSION QUESTIONS

1. Of what are Christians today most often proud?

2. What is the fallacy in measuring self by others?

3. Discuss the seriousness of pride.

4. What are the differences in self-respect and pride? Are Christians to have self-respect?

5. What gifts has God given you? How can you use these for His glory?

6. *Jealously, Envy & Coveteousness*

Jealousy, Envy and Coveteousness are like acids. They do more damage to the vessels in which they are stored, than to the objects on which they are poured.

—paraphrased from Wings of Silver

THE PROBLEM

Satan's largest catches are often made with a three-pronged hook name Jealousy, Envy and Coveteousness. The coveting prong is baited with houses, cars, clothes, travel and exciting life-styles. The envy prong is covered with the looks of a high fashion model, the gifts of a talented friend, and the achievements that would have been yours if given the chance. The jealousy prong is disguised with the confidence that you are a winner, loved and secure.

Satan snagged mankind out of the garden with the prong of coveteousness. He lured Eve to look and then covet the forbidden fruit until she was moved to disobey God. He drove Saul out of his mind with envy of David, and he incited Cain to slay Abel in a jealous rage.

It is doubtful the person lives who has not felt the painful barbs of this three-pronged hook.

The Prong of Jealousy

The dictionary defines jealousy as: (1) intolerant of rivalry or un-faithfulness, (2) disposed to suspect rivalry or unfaithfulness, (3) apprehensive of the loss of another's exclusive affection, and (4) hostile toward a rival or one believed to enjoy an advantage.

As we look at the first definition of jealousy we can understand why God refers to Himself as a jealous God. In Exodus 20:4-6 and other passages, he demands that his people have no other gods before him. And though he is capable of experiencing justified feelings of jealousy, he does not respond to them in a sinful way.

Man on the other hand, does not have a very good record of handling his feelings of jealousy. Of the nine instances where the word is used in the Old Testament, jealousy was either unjustified or responded to sinfully, e.g., Cain of Abel, Sarah of Hagar, Joseph's brethren of Joseph, Saul of David, etc.

A person skewered with jealousy is often driven to illogical and cruel behavior. In 8:6 of the Song of Solomon, jealousy is described as *"cruel as the grave"* and Proverbs 27:4 says, *"Anger is cruel and fury overwhelming but who can stand before jealousy?"* When jealousy controls a person, he is often so frantic he would rather destroy than suffer the knowledge someone else has what he wants.

The Prong of Envy

The dictionary definition of envy is painful and resentful awareness of an advantage enjoyed by another, joined with desire to possess the same advantage.

Feelings of envy are never justified and are always sinful. It is listed as a work of the flesh in Galatians 5:19,20, James warns in 3:16 that its presence will bring about *"every evil practice."* This is understandable when you consider how often envy is the motivation for slander, criticalness, dislike, anger and even hatred.

Seven times we are told not to envy the sinner, which seems surprising until you recall the times you have thought, "It's not fair; they totally ignore God yet look how easy their life is compared to mine." Or the times you have resented yet wanted the achievement, honors, and wealth of people who have perhaps traded their souls for things of the world.

The Prong of Coveteousness

Coveteousness is defined as marked by an inordinate desire for wealth or possessions, or another's possessions, or having a craving for possessions—in other words, greedy.

Colossians 3:5 calls it *idolatry*. And it is—because it longs for and chases after the *things* of this world more than it longs for and chases after the things of God.

A coveting eye is not confined to material possessions alone. It's obvious how all-consuming it can be when God said, *"You shall not covet your neighbor's house. You shall not covet your neighbor's wife, or his manservant or maidservant, his ox or donkey, or anything that belongs to your neighbor."* (Exodus 20:17)

A coveting heart is a heart with the wrong priorities. It is a deceitful heart that whispers, 'This is all you will ever want; as soon as you get this you can relax.' But it cannot keep its promise, for a coveting heart is a *wanting* heart that cannot be filled. Solomon described it in Ecclesiastes 5:10, *"Whoever loves money never has money enough; whoever loves wealth is never satisfied with his income."*

THE SOLUTION

Jealousy, envy, and coveteousness are *inside* sins that motivate us to *outside* sins. They are particularly dangerous because they feed where you are the most vulnerable—the very core of your being—your heart. You can be aware of their presence and burn with shame and yet be unable to free yourself of Satan's pull. David knew he was incapable of freeing himself when he asked God in Psalm 119:36, *"Turn my heart toward your statutes and not toward selfish gain."* For that is where freedom is—in God's statutes. It is available to all who are willing to submit to God.

Overcoming Jealousy

Under certain circumstances, feeling jealous is justified. Just as feeling frightened, happy, sad or angry is justified under certain circumstances. For example, to see your spouse passionately kissing another person would trigger justified feelings of jealousy. This is the jealousy God experiences when he sees his creation involved with idols. Justified feelings of jealousy should motivate us to 'deal' with the problem by turning to God for our options and then acting on those options.

Regardless of whether your jealousy is justified or not, God's teachings will help you understand and deal with the feelings.

Recognize Suspicion For What It Is

Much of man's jealousy is based on suspicion. It's important to learn to recognize it for what it is—your fears, your evil desires, your past experiences.

Suspicion is often simple fear, fear of what they will do, fear of what they are doing, fear of what others will think, fear you are not loved, etc. Suspicious fear should be illegal. Even our laws say a person is innocent until proven guilty. Fear says, 'I'm afraid he is guilty, so he must prove to me he is innocent.'

Suspicion is often based on your own evil desires. It is easy to suspect others of what you do, what you have done, or what you want to do. For example, it is easier to believe someone would steal from the cash register if you have stolen from the cash register, or lie if you have lied.

Suspicion is sometimes the watchdog acquired after an unhappy experience. But all its barking and watching simply boil down to keeping a record of wrong. This attitude does not imitate the *forgiveness and forgetfulness* exhibited by God.

One of the main hang-ups in overcoming any type of suspicion is the age-old question, *What if they make a fool of me?* But remember the age-old answer—*only you can do that.* If someone committed to you is going to become involved with someone else, all your policing, accusing and suspecting will not stop it.

All suspicion displays a certain lack of love. Therefore, the only way you can overcome it is to practice sincerely I Corinthians 13:4-7. And give particular attention to verse 7, *"It (love) always protects, always trusts, always hopes, always perseveres."*

Break the Cycle of Insecurity

A jealous person is usually a very insecure person caught up in a cycle of insecurity. To meet his needs for security, he desperately demands and pressures others for their undivided attention; but the more he pressures, the more he drives others away, and the more they pull away, the more urgently the jealous person pressures—and on and on in an endless cycle of insecurity. Lasting security can only be built on God. It cannot be based on someone else's devotion to you.

But you can break the insecurity cycle by becoming secure. You can do so by *giving* security. It is impossible to *get* security, but it is possible to *give* it, and in giving it to others, you will become secure yourself. Consider the principle on which this is based in Galatians 6:7. *"A man reaps what he sows."* If you would reap security —sow it.

Jealousy and Simple Selfishness

There is an element of simple selfishness in unjustified jealousy. Its possessiveness feeds its ego by dominating and controlling. It is very manipulative and will go to almost any length to retain its control. Dealing with this type of jealousy is as simple as dealing with a selfish child. It must not be catered to and must learn to give instead of take. I Corinthians 10:24 gives you a valuable tool for fighting this type of jealousy in your life, *"Nobody should seek his own good, but the good of others."* That's the secret, seeking the good of others. Choose one person a week that you can help, e.g., an elderly person, a shut-in, a hospital patient, a neighbor and then get busy helping them. Stay so busy that self can't get a jealous thought in edgewise.

Jealousy and a Rival

The jealousy you feel toward a rival is fear someone else will get something you have or want (job, position, honor, etc.) In dealing with this type of jealousy, it is important to review your motive, goal, and purpose. The Jewish leaders had lost sight of these when they were caught up in their jealousy of Christ. Their purpose had become the praise of men, their motive and goal to gain honor and preeminence. Only one thing can overcome this type of jealousy—a return to your original commitment. *"...if anyone would come after me, he must deny himself and take up his cross and follow me."* (Matthew 16:24-25)

Overcoming Envy

It would be nice if feelings of envy set off an alarm that flashed: spiritual immaturity (I Peter 2:1-2), worldliness (I Corinthians 3:3), lack of love (I Corinthians 13:4), and all systems activated to free you from Satan's prong of envy. But God did not create robots; he created men. Then he offered them freedom from envy through his teachings.

Envy and Spiritual Immaturity

I Peter 2:1 lists envy as one of the attributes of a person who has not grown spiritually. The same passage gives a treatment for this condition, *"Therefore, putting aside all malice and all guile and hypocrisy and envy and all slander, like new born babies, long for the pure milk of the word, that by it you may grow..."* (NAS) He is simply saying that to outgrow envy, one must spend time in the Word. Just as a physical baby must be fed consistently, adequately and appropriately to grow, a spiritual baby must be fed consistently, adequately and appropriately to grow.

Envy and Prayer

Matthew 5:44 teaches you how to behave toward an enemy. Anyone you envy is your enemy, not because *he* behaves as an enemy, but because *you* feel toward him as you would an enemy.

By exercising Matthew 5:44 you can change your feelings, *"But I tell you: love your enemies and pray for those who persecute you."* Praying consistently for someone makes you his benefactor and changes your attitude toward him. Does that sound too simple? God has always chosen simple methods to deal with sins we consider too complex to overcome.

Envy and Comparison

It seems the major cause of envy is comparison. We consistently compare our appearance, talents and achievements with other people's appearance, talents and achievements. To overcome Envious Comparison you must develop two new focuses.

The first is the **Fact-Focus.** Has the person you envy accomplished something you want? How did he do it? Are you willing to pay the same price? Examples: (1) If he is thinner than you, it is probably because he eats less or exercise more; which are you willing to do? (2) Does he have a better knowledge of scripture; then he is studying more. Are you willing to put in the time? (3) Does he have an academic degree you envy? Are you willing to go to school? Most skills are learned and most achievements earned, while envy wants something for nothing. Remember, *"A man reaps what he sows."* (Galatians 6:7)

The second focus, when mature, will totally free you from the sin of envy. It is called the **Christ-Focus.** If your attention is locked on Christ, you will have no time or occasion for envious comparison. The only valid comparison for a Christian is comparison to Christ, to the person he was, the things he taught, and the life he lived. We must be busy patterning after him as he patterned after God. *"...I tell you the truth, the Son can do only what he sees his Father doing, because whatever the Father does the Son also does."* (John 5:19)

Overcoming Coveteousness

There is no greater temptation to man than coveteousness. Where jealousy and envy are painful emotions to experience, coveting is often pleasant, robbing you of your *will* to overcome. Who has not experienced the bittersweet pleasure of *wanting* and even found it more exciting than *having*. But the pain of coveting will come with its consequences, i.e., Eve being cast from the garden.

A Formula For Avoiding Coveteousness

Matthew 6:33 provides a formula to avoid coveteousness, *"Seek first His kingdom and His righteousness and all these things shall be given to you also."* See the formula: a command, a priority, a purpose and a promise.

The Command—Seek. It's an action word meaning to go in search of, strive for, look for, try to get. To fulfill this command we must acquire information, apply energy, discipline and focus. It leaves very little time for being tempted by coveteousness.

The Priority—First. God gives the *seeking* a priority. This is what coveteousness usually upsets. Often the things we want are not sin until they are wanted with the wrong priority. The parable of the great banquet in Luke 14 is an example. The guests were invited, the banquet prepared, but when it was time to come, excuses were sent regarding cattle, land and even a wife. None of these things were wrong until they stood between the guests and their invitation from the Lord. As long as you submit to God's priorities, *things* cannot come between you and Him.

A Purpose—The Kingdom and His Righteousness. To live, man must have a purpose. If he doesn't have the right one, he will have a wrong one. When your purpose is the one God chooses for you, *things* will lose their overwhelming allure.

A Promise—All These Things Shall Be Given. *All these things* refers to the clothing, food and lodging that Jesus pointed out God provided for nature. (Matthew 6:26-29) This is a promise that everything you need you will get without anxiety and worry on your part. But it is not an excuse for laziness. Nature is provided for, but at the same time it is busy glorifying God.

Any Christian conscientously applying Matthew 6:33 will not

have the time or the opportunity to live the life of coveteousness described in Matthew 6:32, *"For the pagans run after all these things...."*

The Treasure—Love Circle

In Matthew 6:19-24 Jesus taught about treasures on earth and treasures in heaven. In verse 21 he makes a profound statement, *"For where your treasure is, there your heart will also be."* In other words, what you work for you love, and what you love you work for. What a beautiful and reassuring thought. If you want to love the things of God, work for them. Consider the love and labor of a mother for a child. Which came first, the love or the labor? It's a circle. So working for heavenly treasures will produce love for heavenly treasures instead of things of the world.

DISCUSSION QUESTIONS

1. What point in this lesson had the greatest impact on you? Why?

2. Of the three (jealousy, envy, covetousness), which is the greatest temptation to you? Could one of the points in the lesson help you in the future? How?

3. Think about it a minute then name at least 3 specific sins that could grow out of either jealousy, envy or coveteousness.

4. Explain why all three sins are so closely related to selfishness.

7. Rebellious Heart

"Submit to one another out of reverence for Christ."

—Ephesians 5:21

THE PROBLEM

•A two-year old refuses to obey his mother's command to pick up the blocks.

•A seven-year old declares her independence by insisting upon wearing a different outfit than the one her mother had selected for her.

•A fourteen-year old consistently arrives at the table five full minutes after the rest of the family has assembled.

All of these actions are displays of natural childish rebellion and are expected in normal family living. As the years pass and with proper training, the rebellion also passes. It is another of the childish things Paul refers to in I Corinthians 13:11. *"When I was a child, I talked like a child, I thought like a child, I reasoned like a child. When I became a man, I put childish ways behind me."* And adults never have a problem with this childish trait of rebellion. Right? Wrong! This is something you will have to fight all of your life.

People display rebellion in a variety of ways.

•You don't like the 55 mph speed limit, so you drive 65 mph.

•You are angry at your mate, so you *forget* to do an errand.

- You feel unappreciated, so you spend the day reading instead of doing the cleaning you planned.

- You didn't want the education committee to order a particular set of materials, so when they did you quit teaching.

What Is Rebellion?

Rebellion is defiance or opposition to an established authority. It can be an open demonstration of defiance or it can be a covert, subtle resistance. Rebellion is exercising *won't* power.

Rebellion comes when you feel some right has been violated, when you disagree with a decision, when you feel threatened, when progress is too slow, or when you just want to declare your individuality.

Throughout history Satan has presented rebellion as a *desirable* trait. One false premise accepted by the world is that change can come only by this means. Many social changes have come through the rebellion of a dissatisfied group. Even the birth of our nation was based on rebellion. During the decade of the 60's open rebellion was a popular way to make complaints heard and to effect changes. But all this does not prove that rebellion is the only way, or even the best way, to bring about improvement. The better ways take longer and require more effort and discipline, something most people would rather by-pass.

The place of rebellion in God's sight needs to be determined particularly in regard to attitudes toward those in any kind of authority. Recently, I read a bumper sticker that said, "Question Authority." This seems to be the way of Americans as well as those in other countries today. However, it is not God's way.

Pressures From Women's Groups

Rebellion is not a problem for women only, but at the present time, women appear to have more pressure to rebel and fewer safety valves to prevent it.

Much discontentment has been spawned by the various *radical* women's groups who are actively trying to reorganize the structure God has given. Although women have suffered some injustices, much of the commotion centers around the woman's basic role. Many women have become angry and frustrated with their position in the family and in the church, as well as in the business world. Many have the nagging feeling that women are unappreciated and that maybe their work is not worthwhile. This is fanned by the media—newspaper articles, magazine features, and TV specials and weekly *comedy* shows. Even though a woman may not be in sympathy with the rebellion of the movement, it often influences her thinking more than she realizes. When she begins to feel that *the system* God has established is unfair or that she has as much right to be the head of the house as her husband or that she should be given the leadership at church because she is better qualified, her thinking has been influenced by these attitudes.

Subtle Rebellion

Some Christians practice a *subtle* form of rebellion through the manipulation of a mate, of fellow-workers, or of church leaders.

It is sad to see a situation where a woman is dominating her husband through manipulation. Others can plainly see what is happening. In many situations, even the husband knows what is going on, but it is easier for him to pretend blindness than to fight an invisible enemy. For example, one woman who wanted to move told her husband (who was satisfied where he was), "I know *you* would prefer a warmer climate. I'm happy here, but I'll move with you." The poor man had no intention of moving, but through the years she kept expressing that line of thought. Finally, he did move and she told her friends, "I really didn't want to move, but you know John. When he has an idea, we all have to go along with it." This was blatant manipulation and many women are tempted to use it. Wanting and working for change **is not** sinful. Being unable to accept a decision by an authority in your life **is** sinful.

Another area where subtle rebellion emerges is in relationship to church leadership. This is a danger particularly for involved active women. "The men are not doing this, so someone has to take charge" is a common justification. It is a delicate balance to be able to encourage congregational leaders to move forward without usurping their authority or rebelling against their decisions by ignoring them, by-passing them, or grumbling about them.

Rebellion boils down to an attitude problem. Women can and must have initiative and an active ministry, but it must be done in a spirit of respect, I Timothy 5:17, and of humility. *"Young men (women), in the same way be submissive to those who are older. Clothe yourselves with humility toward one another, because God opposes the proud but gives grace to the humble."* I Peter 5:5.

Impotent Rebellion

Rebellion at events over which one has no control can be very frustrating and can leave an empty feeling of impotence. Such things as job loss, illness, disasters from nature, death, and even daily interruptions can crowd in and leave frustration and anger in their wake. Following the frustration and anger comes rebellion. This is usually a rebellion against God. When no one around can be handily blamed, then God himself becomes the scapegoat. The attitude becomes, "If you have treated me this way, how can you expect me to serve you."

Rebellion Against Own Higher Nature

Paul experienced the revolt of his own nature. When he wanted to do right, his lower self rebelled, resulting in an inner battle, *"So I find this law at work: When I want to do good, evil is right there with me. For in my inner being I delight in God's law; but I see another law at work in the members of my body, waging war against the law of my mind and making me a prisoner of the law of sin at work within my members."* Romans 7:21-23.

Each Christian has these same feelings. Only daily training and constant diligence enable one to *live by the spirit* so that rebellion of the lower nature can be conquered. *"So I say, live by the Spirit, and you will not gratify the desires of the sinful nature. For the sinful nature desires what is contrary to the Spirit, and the Spirit what is contrary to the sinful nature. They are in conflict with each other so that you do not do what you want."* Galatians 5:16,17.

THE SOLUTION

Radical heart surgery is required to remove a rebellious heart. It must be by-passed with submission.

In today's language, submission has become an unpopular word connoting milquetoast and oppression. However, according to the Bible, submission is an active, strong characteristic. It is not a negative role but rather a positive action.

One descriptive phrase is *aggressively submissive*. Submission is a matter of choice. There must be a decision to develop submission; then practice must follow as in developing any skill or trait. Even when feelings are rebellious, exercise of the will can cause submissive actions. With repeated practice of this progression, the feelings begin to correspond with the action, and rebellion erupts much less often.

Areas of Submission

When making choices, each individual must consider the accompanying lifestyle it involves. An athlete must be prepared for a lifestyle of discipline and regular practice. A doctor accepts long years of training and irregular hours as a part of his life. Parents realize that caring for the new baby in their lives requires loss of sleep, loss of privacy, and enormous responsibility. So, also, one who chooses Christianity must acknowledge areas of submission as part of his lifestyle.

1. The first is *to God*. *"Submit yourselves, then to God..."* James

4:7 His will must be sought for the Christian's life. All future decisions are made on this basis: What is God's will for me in this situation?

Total submission to the will of another being, even God Himself, is difficult. Each one of us wants to be *in control* of our actions, but God demands to have that right. However, after experiencing the peace and enriched life that come with submission to God, it is hard to remember the struggle involved in letting him take over the throne. You will wonder why you fought so hard against total submission to God.

2. Christians are instructed to submit to *church leaders. "Obey your leaders and submit to their authority. They keep watch over you as men who must give an account. Obey them so that their work will be a joy, not a burden, for that would be of no advantage to you."* Hebrews 13:17 Theirs is an awesome responsibility—that of overseeing the souls of others—somewhat comparable to that of parenting. How much easier their task when fellow Christians understand and obey this admonition.

3. When electing to marry, Christians also elect submission to one another. *"Submit to one another out of reverence for Christ."* Ephesians 5:21 However, wives have a special responsibility in this area. The final submission rests with them. *"Wives, submit to your husbands as to the Lord. For the husband is the head of the wife as Christ is the head of the church, his body, of which he is the Savior. Now as the church submits to Christ, so also wives should submit to their husbands in everything."* Ephesians 5:22-24 *"Wives, in the same way be submissive to your husbands so that, if any of them do not believe the word, they may be won over without talk by the behavior of their wives."* I Peter 3:1; see also verses 2-6. This is not a burden placed on women, but a joy and release when it is in the context of a Christian marriage. Even without a Christian mate, a wife will find God's plan for her submission works! God, who created women and created her natural tendencies, also created the plan whereby they are expressed and met.

70

4. There is a need to submit one's will to that of *other Christians*. *"Do nothing out of selfish ambition or vain conceit, but in humility consider others better than yourselves. Each of you should look not only to your own interests, but also to the interests of others."* Philippians 2:3,4 When the emphasis is shifted from self to another, this submission comes easily and naturally. No longer are rights demanded, but responsibility and service are sought. Hurt feelings, bruised egos, and friction disappear.

5. The *civil government* also has a right to a Christian's submission. *"Everyone must submit himself to the governing authorities, for there is no authority except that which God has established. The authorities that exist have been established by God. Consequently, he who rebels against the authority is rebelling against what God has instituted, and those who do so will bring judgment on themselves."* Romans 13:1,2 This provides order, continuity, peace, and even furtherance of God's plan. When a civil leader or ruler is seen as an instrument of God as described in Romans, there is no question as to his right for honor and obedience. *"Therefore, it is necessary to submit to the authorities, not only because of possible punishment but also because of conscience."* Romans 13:5

Christ's Submission

The extreme example of one being submissive to another is seen in Christ. He submitted to his parents (Luke 2:51), to religious requirements (Luke 2:41,42), to his followers (John 13:12-15), to his enemies (John 18:4-8), and even to death for those of all the ages. *"But made himself nothing, taking the very nature of a servant, being made in human likeness. And being found in appearance as a man, he humbled himself and became obedient to death—even death on a cross!"* Philippians 2:7,8 If our Lord humbled himself in all these ways, why is it so hard for Christians to do the same? *"Your attitude should be the same as that of Christ Jesus."* Philippians 2:5

71

DISCUSSION QUESTIONS

1. Discuss Christ's attitude of submission.

2. Discuss how you rebel in these areas:
   God
   Church leaders
   Husbands
   One another
   Civil authorities

3. When do you find rebelliousness welling up in yourself most often? How can you change your attitude at these times?

8. Self-Image 1

"I would know myself better, if there weren't so many of me."

—Wings of Silver

THE PROBLEM

Have you ever heard someone say:
* *I have the worst self-image.*
* *My biggest problem is my self-image.*
* *I can't do anything because my self-image is so poor.*

Or perhaps you have:
* *Felt so inferior you were sure even God didn't like you.*
* *Lashed out at others because you were so disgusted with yourself.*
* *Found yourself boasting desperately to make a good impression.*

All of these are symptoms of self-image problems.*

Your self-image influences every area of your life. It affects the way you respond to family, friends, opportunities, situations and even to God. It can affect the amount of conflict you have with others and the amount of inner conflict you have with yourself. It

---

*For the purpose of this study, the commonly understood definition of good/bad self-image will be used. Bad self-image meaning feelings of inferiority and dislike; good self-image meaning self-liking and respect.

can determine whether you live with self-respect or self-reproach. It can void every success in your life and magnify every failure. It can give you the strength to try again or make you surrender without trying at all.

In the last few years society has become very self-image conscious. It considers a good self-image the primary explanation for success—and a bad self-image the automatic reason for unhappiness and failure. For many, obtaining a good self-image has become a major concern in life.

After devoting a great deal of time to studying self-image problems behaviorial scientists have developed a variety of methods and formulas for cultivating a good self-image. Almost all of these techniques are based on two major principles: (1) experiencing positive reinforcement, and (2) liking yourself.

Experiencing positive reinforcement can be explained simply as getting a pat on the back. To have a good self-image, you must get pats on the back, but to do so you need a good self-image. If that sounds like a circle, it is. It could be illustrated like this:

$$\left(\begin{array}{c} \text{good self-image} \\ \text{pats on the back} \end{array} \right)$$

But how do you get started on such a successful merry-go-round? Your parents or some other supportive force in your life can put you on this upward spiral. But if they don't, you can enter through various aspects of positive thinking.

Sounds good, doesn't it? And it very often works. On the other hand, it very often doesn't work because some important ingredients are missing.

Liking yourself is also a must according to man's self-image program. If there are things about yourself that you cannot like, they are considered hang-ups. To overcome your hangups you must (a) accept yourself the way you are, (b) get rid of any feelings of guilt, and (c) adjust your values until they are realistic for you. It seems reasonable until you realize that it means change your values to match your behavior.

Liking yourself and feeling valuable are also important parts of God's self-image program, but God and man differ on how to accomplish it.

How Successful Is Man's Self-Image Program

Man's formula does not always cure self-image problems, but he has some reasonable sounding explanations when it fails: (1) you were criticized too much as a child, (2) you have been rejected and abused until your self-esteem has been destroyed.

On the other hand, man's formula often experiences a degree of success, which is easily understood when you realize it coincides in several aspects with God's program. Unfortunately, though, it leaves out or distorts some basic fundamentals.

THE SOLUTION

It may seem strange to say God has a solution for self-image problems when the word *self-image* does not appear in the Bible. But God deals with self-image problems as he does a multitude of others. He approaches them very simply by: (1) teaching you the truth concerning the situation, and (2) training you to avoid or overcome the problem in the future.

The first principle, TRUTH FREES, is based on John 8:32. In this passage Jesus tells his disciples that by knowing the truth they can be free. At the time, he was referring specifically to being free from sin. But the principle is applicable to a multitude of situations. For example, knowing the truth and living by it can free you from traffic tickets, lung cancer resulting from smoking cigarettes, or a black eye from picking a fight with someone a lot bigger than you. God frees you from self-image problems by teaching some basic truths that apply to self-image problems.

The second principle, GOD'S INSTRUCTION PROTECTS AND DEVELOPS, is founded on 2 Timothy 3:16,17. There Paul teaches that through scripture you can be taught, corrected, trained, well-prepared and fully equipped for every good work. With such instructions you can have a good productive life that develops a glowing self-image.

Your House of Mirrors

To better understand self-image problems, imagine yourself building a house for self-inspection to be filled with mirrors. If you carefully select each mirror you install and make sure it is absolutely accurate, you will be able to step into the room and from any angle get an honest reflection of yourself. That is what your self-image is—your reflection as seen by you. Then anything in your reflection you do not like, you can alter by changing yourself. For example, if your image is too fat, go on a diet. If your image has temper tantrums, start controlling your anger. And if your mirrors are perfect, this lesson can end with this conclusion—what you don't like about your image, transform by changing yourself.

But unfortunately you often include some imperfect mirrors in your house of self-inspection which distort your image, giving you a false reflection to work with. It is these distorted images that are the source of many self-image problems.

In this study we will work with some of the most commonly distorted mirrors, regrinding them with truth. Then you can reevaluate your image in these corrected mirrors as you take shape under God's instruction.

Correct Vision Through Self-Acceptance

To work realistically on your image in your house of self-inspection, you must have correct vision. For no matter how accurate the mirrors, without correct vision you will perceive a distorted reflection.

The basis for correct vision is acceptance of your heritage (or roots). God created you and gave you the freedom of choice in many areas of your life. But one choice he withheld, the selection of your roots (heritage) which includes your natural parents and grandparents, your natural appearance, your natural aptitudes (abilities), and your social and ethnic background. The rejection of any one of these roots makes it impossible to see yourself realistically because you are blocking out a portion of your image. However, by applying God's truth and instruction you can develop acceptance and respect for your heritage resulting in realistic self-vision.

The Root of Natural Appearance

The root you most often reject or refuse to see realistically is natural appearance. Very seldom will you answer, "Nothing," when asked what you would change about your appearance. But, if you have a good self-image, you would simply be saying your appearance could be improved. However, if you have a poor self-image, you could mean everything from general dissatisfaction with your looks to actual self-hatred.

The Truth: Outward beauty cannot by itself bring inner happiness or a good self-image. In fact, Proverbs 31:30 tells us that outward beauty is deceitful (it can temporarily cover inner ugliness, thus deceiving) and vain (because it gives a false pride). Real beauty only comes from within (I Peter 3:4) with a quiet and gentle spirit. The man who brought salvation to the world was not outwardly beautiful (Isaiah 53:2), but his inner beauty guaranteed that he was never forgotten or ever ignored. By this same token, if you wish to be beautiful and remembered, develop inner beauty.

God's Instruction: God's instruction develops a new countenance, self-acceptance, appearance and appreciation. Conforming to Ephesians 4:17-5:20 cultivates a radiant inner beauty and following Proverbs 31:10-31 develops a beauty that grows with each passing year.

The Root of Parentage

At sometime (often in early teens) you are usually embarrassed, ashamed or in some way reject your parents. But as you mature, that attitude should change to one of acceptance. If it doesn't, you'll find you cannot accept yourself because, like it or not, they are a part of you.

The Truth: There are many excuses for dishonor, disobedience, or rejection of parents, but only one explanation—sin. The sin of pride causes you to be ashamed of a parent's poverty, lack of education, appearance, social graces, etc. The sin of rebellion causes you to be disrespectful and contemptuous of their authority, while an unforgiving heart causes bitterness, resentment and even hatred for actual or imagined wrongs. Dishonor of parents really has nothing to do with a parent's worthiness or unworthiness—it has to do with your heart.

God's Instruction: *"Children, obey your parents in the Lord, for this is right. Honor your father and mother—which is the first commandment with a promise—that it may go well with you and that you may enjoy long life on the earth."* (Ephesians 6:1-3) This command appears to benefit only the parent, but the blessing of obedience to God is always multi-faceted. It is pleasant for a parent to have an obedient, respectful child, but it is critical for the child to be respectful and obedient. Obedience protects a child from conflict, foolish decisions, physical trauma, ignorant mistakes, etc., while at the same time it trains him to respect authority, trust others, be teachable, not to be self-willed, etc. He will find the more respect he gives the authority figures in his life, the more respect he will have for himself. Invariably the child (or adult child) that does not esteem his parents will not esteem himself.

The Roof of Natural Abilities

If you have a good self-image, you accept your natural gifts and abilities with a degree of thankfulness and appreciation. If you have a poor self-image you are probably convinced you do not have any gifts or abilities. And if one is pointed out, you more than likely answer incredulously, "You call that a gift; anyone can do that."

The Truth: You (and everyone else) have been given natural gifts and talents for specific purposes. (Romans 12:3-8; I Corinthians 12:12-26) Your attitude about those talents plays a major role in your self-image. If you have a good self-image, you are probably busy exercising and multiplying your gifts. If you have a poor self-image, you are probably ignoring your talents and longing for someone else's. (See chapter on **Envy**)

God's Instruction: Two of God's basic commands can help you overcome this source of self-image problems. The first, *"...give thanks in all circumstances; for this is the will of God in Christ Jesus for you."* (1 Thessalonians 5:18, RSV) Try it; thank God for each gift or talent, even those that seem trivial. You will find even as you utter your thanks, you will receive insight into its potential. For example, "Thank you God that I have been taught how to cook. I realize I can use it to please my family, exercise hospitality, take meals to the sick, train my daughters, write a cookbook, and even teach a cooking class for children." As you thank God, you will see your talents in a new perspective.

The second command, *"Whatever your task, work heartily, as serving the Lord and not men."* (Colossians 3:23) Any job you perform, no matter how trivial, affects your self-image because it reflects your worth. As a result, your self-image is based more on how you perform than what you perform. So God teaches you to attack every job heartily. For example, compare the dreariness and fatigue of weeding a flower bed *reluctantly* to the pride and joy of a freshly weeded bed you've attacked cheerfully. Nothing enhances your self-image more than the satisfaction of a job well done. In this command God gives Christians the motivation (as serving the Lord) to exercise every talent, task and chore with enthusiasm.

The Root of Social, Ethnic, Racial Background

As a person you often have difficulty being comfortable unless everyone else is just like you. Frequently, your response to this uncomfortableness is to develop prejudices—racial, ethnic, social, etc. When those prejudices are directed at others, they are bigotry. When they are directed at your own racial, ethnic, or social status, they are even more damaging because they bring about self-rejection.

The Truth: God deals with this problem by removing every source of difference. In Galatians 3:26-28 we read, *"You are all sons of God through faith in Christ Jesus, for all of you who were baptized into Christ have been clothed with Christ. There is neither Jew nor Greek, slave nor free, male nor female, for you are all one in Christ Jesus. If you belong to Christ, then you are Abraham's seed, and heirs according to the promise."* This scripture reminds me of a parent with a group of children who are quarreling over who gets to be superman. He solves the argument by declaring all of them superman. God has decreed that in Christ you are all sons. Your spiritual birth which supercedes your physical birth transposes you into a spiritual realm where there is no social, ethnic, racial or sexual difference. The next chapter goes on to talk of the difference between an heir and a slave and in Galatians 4:7 he says, *"So you are no longer a slave, but a son; and since you are a son, God has made you also an heir."* If your social, ethnic, or racial background is controlling your reactions to God and others, then you are thinking like a slave instead of a son.

God's Instruction: Romans 13:8-10, *"Let no debt remain outstanding, except the continuing debt to love one another, for he who loves his fellow man has fulfilled the law...Love does no harm to its neighbor. Therefore love is the fulfillment of the law."* In this passage we are told our responsibility is to love our fellow man. Colossians 3:12-14 gives some specific ways we can behave toward our fellow man, i.e., compassionate, kind, humble, gentle, patient, and forgiving. The passage concludes with, *"And over all these virtues put on love, which binds them all together in perfect unity."* By putting love on (something you can choose to do) you bind all your behaviors together in a perfect unity that crosses racial, ethnic and social barriers.

Your Roots, God's Picture Frame

You are God's creation; you didn't just happen. According to Psalms 139:13-16 you were designed by God. He created you just like every other man and yet unlike any other man. Part of your uniqueness is your roots.

When an artist creates a painting, he does not just slap it into any frame. Instead he selects the "right" frame to bring out the colors, texture, and perspective of his painting so it will better illustrate his message. That is what God has done with you and your heritage.

Have you known people that appeared rather average until you knew their background? Then they became an inspiration to you. Your heritage is the frame selected to display your message to the world. And because of your uniqueness there are people who will hear you in a way they would not hear others. An example of this is found in Acts 4:13. In that instance the Sanhedrin was astonished at Peter's presentation because he lacked education, was from a provincial area, and was just a fisherman. However, it was these very things that gave Peter's message power and brought credit to Jesus, *"...they took note he had been with Jesus."*

Consider the frame God chose for the Savior of the world. He did not send him with the best education, great wealth, or a position of prominence (all of the "advantages"). Instead he sent him with no particular attractiveness (Isaiah 53:2), no special education, a birth veiled in disgrace, and the social background of a craftsman. Yet Christ did not suffer self-image problems because he knew his mission and was confident of his relationship with God. These happen to be the two greatest defenses against self-image problems— knowing your purpose and being secure in your relationship with God.

Seeing your heritage realistically and accepting it is the foundation for your self-image. If not viewed realistically, it will not only create self-image problems, but it will distort other situations that can also create self-image problems. So before proceeding to the next portion of this study be certain you resolve any conflict you might have with any area of your heritage (God's special roots for you).

The next chapter, Self-Image II, is a continuation of this chapter. It will deal with the distorted mirrors that cause many self-image problems.

9. Self-Image II

QUESTION: *How successful would a cake be if you left the flour out of*
the recipe?

ANSWER: *As successful as this chapter will be if you attempt to study*
it without studying Self-Image I!

THE PROBLEM

The information in Self-Image I is like the flour or base for Self-Image II. It notes man's awareness of self-image problems and explains the principles in God's solution. It also applies those principles to the foundation of your self-image, your heritage.

This chapter will pick up where the last chapter left off and deal with the distorted mirrors mentioned in Part I. Recall, in that portion you learned your self-image is merely your reflection as seen by you. Therefore, what you don't like in your image, change by changing yourself. This method can effectively deal with self-image problems unless you are inspecting yourself in a distorted mirror.

The Distorted Mirror of Past Sin

A poor self-image often originates from not having your past life in the proper perspective. You can always recall behavior that makes you burn with shame. Frequently, that behavior was so repulsive and unjustified that it is painfully and eternally seared in your mind's eye. And every time you look at your reflection you only see the person that behaved in that manner.

The Truth: If you are a Christian, God murdered the image you are looking at. He/she was crucified on the cross (Galatians 2:20), buried with Christ (Romans 6), and raised to a new life (a new way) to live, a new way to talk, a new way to behave, and a new way to think).

If you experienced that death, burial and resurrection, and yet you are still struggling with your old self-image, it is probably because you have dug up the corpse and are dragging it around with you. Naturally, the stench of that dead body will make it difficult and unpleasant to live your new life. You must let God bury it under the truth—and this is the truth—the old you is dead. Now let it return to the dust *"from whence it came."*

If your self-image problems originate in sins you've committed since you became a Christian, repent and accept God's gift of forgiveness. Take advantage of Hebrews 8:12 where God promises to remember your sins no more. And rejoice that Christ's blood is continually cleansing you (1 John 1:7).

God's Instruction: Your bad self-image resulted from your past behavior (the things you did, said and thought). But that is over. God is now patiently instructing you for your new self-image. He has outlined if for you in Ephesians 4:17-5:20. And as you submit to his guidance, you cannot help but develop as a child of light (Ephesians 5:8) with a radiant self-image.

The Distorted Mirror of Self-Expectations

Frequently, self-expectations are a source of self-image problems. When unfilfilled, they can keep you living and thinking as a failure and are responsible for self-anger and self-disgust.

Self-expectations should *not* be confused with self-confidence or self-goals. Self-confidence is the belief you are capable of achievement. A self-goal is an end you have chosen for yourself, while a self-expectation is something you expect to do, be or get. Time and again what starts out as self-confidence or a self-goal becomes a demanding self-expectation. If you don't live up to that expectation, you see yourself as a failure, thus creating self-image problems.

Any self-expectation has the potential to create problems but the ones that almost invariably trigger self-image problems are: the *unfilfilled* and the *unrealistic*.

The *unfulfilled* expectation can be recognized by its accompanying disappointment. Your life may be permeated with unfulfilled expectations and you be unaware of it. Test yourself by listening to the way you talk or think, "I am so disappointed with myself over this or over that, because of this or because of that, etc." If that is your thinking, your various wants and wishes have become self-expectations and when unfulfilled they become one disappointment after another, giving the illusion of failure.

Unrealistic expectations (because they usually remain unfulfilled) often create feelings of failure which have a strong impact on your self-image. Unrealistic expectations don't just challenge you but run ahead of your abilities and accomplishments, always keeping you in the shadows of failure.

Self-Expectations are unrealistic when they are:

(1) based on someone else's abilities, circumstances, etc. For example, you cannot expect to be a gifted vocalist, straight A student, and the local beauty because your mother or best friend's aunt was. (You may be all of those things, but you cannot assume you will be.)

(2) based on wishful thinking instead of a workable plan. For example, you cannot expect to know the Bible well by wanting to know it well, talking about knowing it well, thinking about knowing it well, and getting angry at yourself because you don't know it well. You must sit down and get into it.

(3) beyond your ability or skills to perform. If you are 5'2" and weigh 97 pounds you cannot expect to play football for the Dallas Cowboys, or if you have never learned to drive you cannot expect to be hired as a Greyhound bus driver (without learning to drive first).

The Truth: God teaches us to *strive* toward goals, not *expect*. You can easily understand why when you realize *to strive* is to work toward, while *to expect* is to depend on someone (yourself) fulfilling. When you *expect,* you are in the market of *getting* when you *strive;* you are in the market of *giving* which is God's way. Even God does not expect of man. He loves man, offers him an abundant life if he submits to his instruction and even forgives him on the occasions he falls short. It seems the only thing God really expects of man—with good cause—is to fall short. This is not a negative attitude toward man or his abilities; instead it is a realistic, generous, and merciful one.

God's Instruction: The attitude displayed by Paul in the Philippian letter gives valuable training in the handling of disappointment, goals and confidence.

(1) Disappointment. Paul's desire for freedom from prison could have become a self-expectation. He wrote time and again to the disciples saying he felt very certain he would be released soon. And each time he wasn't he could have sunk into a depression and abased himself for not convincing the judges to release him, or for his hasty appeal to Caesar that hindered Felix from freeing him, etc. But Philippians 1:12-18 displays his openness to seeing every situation in God's perspective. Paul overcame what could have been disappointment in God and himself by being God oriented instead of self oriented.

(2) Goals. Paul's attitude regarding a goal was one of *"straining and pressing toward"* according to Philippians 3:12-14. In other words, giving it everything he had, aware it would be his if it was God's will.

(3) Confidence. Paul placed his confidence (and expectations) in Christ not himself (vs. 12ff) and was never confronted with failure because when his plans did not work out; God's did (Philippians 1:12-18).

The Distorted Mirror of Self-Pity

Self-pity is an unlikely sounding source of self-image problems, but it can and does create some very serious ones. For if you feel mistreated, you invariably feel of little value. One of the most relentless self-image problems I have ever seen controlled an attractive, successful business woman. She had been rejected by her parents when she became a Christian and rejected by her husband in their marriage. After struggling with both situations for years, she developed among other things a bad case of self-pity, creating a severe self-image problem. If she had responded to those rejections in God's way, her self-image could have survived and she would have grown spiritually as a result of her problems.

The Truth: John 16:33 tells us that, *"...in this world you will have trouble..."* Jesus is saying very plainly in that scripture you will have difficult times, times of unfair and unhappy situations. But 1 Corinthians 10:13 tells you that whatever the circumstances, nothing will happen that has not happened to other people before you. And with every temptation you will be given a way of escape.

God's Instruction: *"Give thanks in all circumstances, for this is God's will for you in Christ Jesus."* (1 Thessalonians 5:18). Obeying this command and practicing it as a principle will protect you from self-pity and its accompanying self-image problems. It will also help you develop insight. A most dramatic example of this was in the case of Joseph in Genesis 45. If any one ever had a right to a little self-pity, Joseph did. He was rejected by family, sold into slavery, thrown into jail when he was innocent, and forgotten by the cellmate he befriended. Yet, Joseph concluded all of this with the remark in Genesis 50:20 when he lovingly said to the brothers who had wronged him, *"...you intended to harm me, but God meant it for good."*

A second example is in Acts 5:40-42. There the apostles were called before the Sanhedrin, told to quit preaching in the name of Jesus, and flogged to reinforce the point. They could have felt mistreated, because they were. But verse 41 says they went out rejoicing because they were counted worthy to suffer for the Lord's name. They could have been miserable, but they were happy because they were viewing the situation God's way.

Very likely both of these examples are a little extreme for the things that will happen to most of us. But the principle is the same and can be applied to every circumstance. For example, a mailman delivers a tax tax refund to 122 E. Anystreet. The woman is thrilled, thanking God for the money to pay an unexpected dental bill. The same mailman delivers a tax refund to 127 E. Anystreet. That woman becomes depressed. She had expected to be able to save a little and buy a few extras. Instead they would have to use it to pay an unexpected dental bill. It didn't seem fair; something always came up to keep them from getting ahead. The situation is identical but the way they view, it is different. One is using God's perspective, grateful for everything, thus she is happy. The other is seeing the situation in man's way and is miserably sinking deeper and deeper in self-pity.

The Distorted Mirror of Weak Faith

Do you know what you should be doing for the Lord, but you're not doing it and consequently you're disgusted with yourself? If so, your weak faith is creating a poor self-image.

The Truth: If you realize you have a poor self-image and it's due to your weak faith (a faith that does not motivate you to be the servant God wants you to be), there is only one way to deal with it — strengthen you faith.

God's Instruction: Colossians 2:6-7 teaches us to strengthen our faith, *"So then, just as you received Christ Jesus as Lord continue to live in him, rooted and built up in him, strengthened in the faith as you were taught and overflowing with thankfulness."* Notice this teaches three things accompany a strengthened faith: (1) continuing to live in him. In other words, you must "hang in there", be steadfast in continuing to live as you did when you first came to know Jesus, (2) being rooted and built up in him. In order to let your roots go down into Christ, you must know him, and that can only happen through his Word and prayer. It is impossible to be rooted and built up apart from the Word of God. (3) Overflowing with thankfulness. Practicing thankfulness trains you to see God's hand in your life, and that perspective strengthens your faith as nothing else can.

Jesus teaches a beautiful and astonishing principle in John 13:17 that will strengthen you faith, you life and your self-image when practiced. *"If you know these things you are blessed if you do them."* Remembering the word *blessed* means "happy," you can understand that the road to happiness is doing what you know to do. Anytime you fall short of doing what you "know to do," you are going to suffer conflict and self-image problems. For example, I know that nothing strengthens me and contributes more to my spiritual growth than a daily devotional time with God. If I neglect that for several days, I begin to feel separated from God and my self-image suffers.

The Distorted Mirror of Rejection and Disapproval

Do you feel something is wrong with you because this person doesn't like you or that person doesn't like you? If so, your self-image is based on the reactions of other people. No one is more miserable or insecure than the person whose self-image is controlled by the reactions of others. The reactions of others are valuable tools, telling you when you are being kind and loving and reminding you when you are being rude or inconsiderate. But they cannot be the basis for your self-image, for "their" reactions are based on "their" distorted mirrors and may not always be truthful or justified.

The Truth: The person does not live who has not faced rejection and disapproval sometime in life. Even Christ was rejected and he had led a sinless life. However, it did not affect his self-image because it was based on God's approval and not man's. If you follow his example, you will find disapproval and rejection can hurt,but they cannot destroy you or a good self-image.

God's Instruction: 1 Peter 2:23 tells us that when Christ was rejected or insulted he "entrusted" himself to God. Have you ever considered how he entrusted himself to God? (1) He put himself in God's protection and accepted what came; (2) He relied on God by responding as God had taught him to, i.e., *"love your enemies...pray for them that despitefully use...do not repay evil for evil...";* and (3) He waited for God instead of reacting man's way, i.e., getting even, wallowing in self-pity, becoming resentful and bitter, etc.

Romans 8:28 gives us valuable insight in following the example of Christs' responses, *"All things work for the good of those that love the Lord."* This teaches (among other things) that there is not a circumstance in your life that cannot work for your good if you respond in the way God teaches you to.

Both scriptures keep your attention focused on your response and God's will, thus putting others reactions to you in proper perspective. With the right focus your self image will be based on God's approval instead of man's.

In Conclusion

At the beginning of this study, we looked at man's solution for self-image problems, experiencing positive reinforcement and liking yourself, which are also part of God's solution. However, God is capable of giving them much greater depth than man. For example, man teaches you to experience success through positive thinking, and then must turn you over to the world for the pats on the back which result from success. But God teaches that each one of his children starts as a success, *"For everyone born of God has overcome the world. This is the victory that has overcome the world, even our faith."* (1 John 5:4) Then he changes your standards of success from those of the world to those in his Word: faith, love, kindness, gentleness, patience, steadfastness, etc. He even trains you in that success — success that the world cannot take away from you. Man wants you to experience success, but he must rely on the world to give it to you which is an "iffy" situation.

God offers you success through a relationship with him which is not "iffy."

God encourages you to think success through the positive thinking approach from Proverbs 23:7, *"As a man thinketh in his heart so is he."* Man interprets this scripture to mean that anything you think (believe) you can do, you can. This is a valid interpretation when qualified with "if it be God's will." What it does positively teach is that your behavior, accomplishment, and goals begin in your mind. Then he promised to aid you with those behaviors, accomplishments and goals. *"Ask and it will be given you; seek and you will find; knock and the door will be opened to you. For everyone who asks receives; he who seeks finds; and to him who knocks, the door will be opened."* (Matthew 7:7-8)

Man teaches "like yourself" — also a portion of God's program but man tries to help you accomplish that by adjusting your *likes* until they fit your *behavior*. God's program recognizes the importance of "liking yourself" and he starts by giving you value and worth through his love. He backs up his love with the death of his son. He teaches you what he would have you be, and then teaches you how to like yourself by being that person. And with that new way to live, he gives you self-respect, self-esteem and self-liking. Man's program teaches you that guilt exists only in your mind, while God's program teaches man what guilt is, how to be free of it, and then reinforces the new you with love and approval by surrounding you with Christians who have been taught, *"love one another as I have loved you,"* (John 13:34) and *"greet one another with a holy kiss."* (1 Corinthians 16:20)

DISCUSSION QUESTIONS

1. What point in this lesson had the most impact on you? Why?

2. What other distorted mirrors can you think of? What would God's truth and instruction be for them?

3. Read Galatians 6:3. What distorted mirror would that man be looking in? How does verse 4 relate?

4. What insight does 2 Corinthians 13:5 give you regarding yourself?

10. Sins of the Tongue

*"The second most deadly instrument of destruction
is the gun — the first is the human tongue."*

— William George Jordan

THE PROBLEM

Let me see your tongue. Have you ever heard a doctor say that? The appearance of the tongue can give a clue to many diseases. The same is true spiritually. A diseased heart may be manifested by a bitter tongue.

The list of "tongue diseases" might be endless, but here four of them will be discussed.

1. Gossip

One of the easiest sins to be involved in is gossip. When you mentally review a recent conversation, have you ever been shocked at the things you said or encouraged another to say? Our conversational patterns lead us into gossip before we realize what is happening. There are some phrases that should alert us. When you say or hear said, "I am telling you this to help her. . .I wouldn't repeat this, but. . .I am only trying to warn you. . . ," and other such expressions that precede a juicy gossip tidbit, you need to check the real motives behind this telling. Most often these introductions to gossip are made merely to make it more palatable.

Why do Christians gossip?

a. It may be an effort to divert attention from one's own sin by directing those around to look at the fault in another. While they are looking away, the sin in one's own life can be hidden or glossed over.

b. It may be an attempt to justify one's own sinful life and to console a biting conscience. Jesus condemned focusing on the faults and sins of others while ignoring our own. *"Why do you look at the speck of sawdust in your brother's eye and pay no attention to the plank in your own eye?"* (Luke 6:41)

c. It may be an attempt to build up self by tearing down another. The Pharisee who prayed thanking God that he was not like the sinner was doing this (Luke 18:9-14). There is always someone about who is worse than you are. It makes you feel holy to compare yourself with that person. It's easy to say to yourself, "Thank God I am not like that."

d. It may be an expression of envy and hatred — the kind that seeks to destroy its victim. This was the motivation of the Jews in Acts 13:45 when they *"talked abusively against what Paul was saying."* While overt action against another is not acceptable, words are permitted to flow freely, even destructive words.

Gossip can be found in the list of things God hates (Proverbs 6:16-19). It is a serious offense.

2. Grumbling and Complaining

"Do everything without complaining or arguing." (Philippians 2:14). The children of Israel were repeatedly chastised for complaining. No matter how bad the previous situation, they felt it was better than the present one. The food was better in Egypt. Even though the Pharoahs mistreated them that was preferable to wandering around in the wilderness. The water was more desirable. On and on they complained. How impatient God must have felt with them, yet he continued to bear with them. Is today different? How impatient he must feel today when he hears our various

grumblings.

This underground murmuring can weaken the foundation of any congregation. Moses lamented, *"Why have you brought this trouble on your servant? What have I done to displease you that you put the burden of all these people on me?"* (Numbers 11:11) When the people murmur, it puts a discouraging load on the leaders. Good programs of work are launched to be forsaken later because of complaints and criticisms. When elders, preachers, and teachers have to spend time fighting the brush fires of murmuring among the Christians, there is little or no time left to fight the enemy — Satan.

3. Lying

Another of the things God hates is a lying tongue. Tempers quickly flare when one is accused of lying, but in everyday life lying is common. A wife will say a gadget costs $3.00 instead of the true $3.98 because she has overspent her budget. A man will report his regular income on tax forms, but not the extras that have come his way that year. Children tell teachers that homework is lost rather than admitting that it was never done. Parents are not shocked nor do they express disapproval when children lie to one another. *Social lying* is accepted as a form of tact. Exaggeration is overlooked.

The very basis of God's word is truth. When Christians lose regard for the truth in everyday life, it will also affect their regard for God's word. They lose a sense of the cost of truth and the value of truth.

4. Sharp or Angry Words

Eversharp may be a good name for a pencil, but it is a poor description for a woman. One quality found in every list describing a good woman is gentleness and kindness. The perfect wife of Proverbs 31 is said to have the *"teaching of kindness"* (RSV) in her tongue. The fruit of the Spirit includes gentleness, kindness and patience (Galatians 5:22,23). Wives are to be adorned with a *"gentle and quiet spirit.* " (1 Peter 3:4) The older women are to teach the younger women to be kind (Titus 2:5).

Verbal abuse is common. People who would never physically harm other humans will freely destroy them with words. It seems to be all right to vent great anger and frustration at your family, at strangers (store clerks, those answering telephones, drivers who inconvenience you) and at people under authority in working situations by giving them a *tongue lashing.*

One area of great concern today is the harm done to children by parents who abuse them emotionally by words. Many children carry into adulthood feelings of incompetence, resentment, and fear as a result of verbal abuse from parents or other adults.

How much harm is done to relationship of all kinds by a quick, angry retort. Homes are broken, children are alienated, friendships are destroyed, and souls are turned away. The beauty of a woman can be hidden by her sharp tongue.

THE SOLUTION

1. A strict accounting of every word for a few days will show where the tongue is causing sin. Just be aware of everything you say and think about it after you are removed from the situation in which you said it. This exercise in examination needs to be done regularly. When you have identified which of the sins of the tongue trouble you, actions against them can be taken.

2. Psalms 19:14, *"May the words of my mouth and the meditation of my heart be pleasing in your sight, O Lord, my Rock and my Redeemer."* needs to become a motto. Pray often for help in controlling the tongue. David was doing just that in this Psalm. James tells us no human can tame the tongue (James 3:8), but we can tame it through the power of Christ. *"I can do everything through him who gives me strength."* (Philippians 4:13)

3. The heart must be filled with goodness in order for goodness to come from the tongue. *"...for out of the overflow of the heart the mouth speaks. The good man brings good things out of the*

good stored up in him, and the evil man brings evil things out of the evil stored up in him." (Matthew 12:34,35) When your mind is filled with bitterness, hatred, jealousy, anger, and selfishness, the tongue will respond in those ways. When the heart is trained in gentleness, kindness, praise, and love, the tongue will express those emotions.

Investing Words

Words need to be treated like money. They should be spent wisely, never wasted, and whenever possible used as an investment. Are you pleased for Christ to know what you are saying? *"But I tell you that men will have to give account on the day of judgment for every careless word they have spoken. For by your words you will be acquitted, and by your words you will be condemned."* (Matthew 12:36,37)

Here are some ways words can be invested:

a. **Praise.** (Romans 14:11; Philippians 2:9-11) How limited is your praise vocabulary? It is difficult to express praise to God because these words are not used enough for them to be readily available in our minds. No amount of praise can be too much. When thoughts are turned to the magnificence of God, the natural result is praise to him. By reading and repeating many of the Psalms, a praise vocabulary can be developed. Many times Paul in his writings bursts into praise; these passages can be used as patterns also.

b. **Encouragement.** (Proverbs 15:23; 25:11) All around you are people starving for encouragement. Great tasks have been undertaken and completed because of a word of encouragement. On the other hand, many more have been abandoned because of discouragement. A little kind praise makes children blossom, mates glow with love, friends rejoice, and fellow workers strive harder. Take time to notice and express encouragement to those special people around you. Even a brief compliment to a clerk on her efficiency can change the course of her day. How much more your family will respond.

c. **Teaching.** (1 Timothy 4:11; Ephesians 4:15) Eternity is in the words of a teacher. Christians are instructed to teach in a variety of ways — by example, parents training children, friends sharing the good news, elders admonishing the church, etc. There is no greater way to use the power of the tongue than in teaching. You are teaching something all the time by your words. Is that *something* what you want to be teaching? Awareness of the power of influence in words will cause you to be most careful that what you are teaching is truth, love, Christ.

Busy Tongues

Busy tongues are not sinful. They can be busy producing good fruit. When this is happening, there is no time or energy left for the sins of the tongue.

DISCUSSION QUESTIONS

1. Read James 3:1-12. How is the tongue described? What harm can come from the tongue?

2. Read Matthew 12:33-37. Are sins of the tongue serious? What causes a sinful tongue?

3. How do you stop gossip in yourself? In those around you?

4. When do you find it most difficult to be kind? How can you alter that situation?

11. Blameshifting

"The fault, dear Brutus, is not in our stars but in ourselves."

— Shakespeare

THE PROBLEM

Blameshifting is as old as mankind. It is just another way of saying *excuse giving.* Since the beginning of time, men and women have looked for ways to alleviate their own guilt by blaming the shortcomings in their lives on someone or something else. People just do not like to face their sins and admit them.

Christians spend a great deal of their lives looking for reasons why they are not living up to the Christian ideal and then spend even more time telling others what those reasons are. It is not only a waste of time, it is sinful. Self-discipline is hard, but it is much easier and much less time-consuming in the long run than looking for ways to excuse sin in self.

Help Is Available to Change

Phrases like, "It's just the way I am" or "I can't seem to help myself" are common ways to excuse behavior, especially behavior that is hard to change. It is true that you can't help yourself. However, you do not have to depend on your own strength to change. God can and will help you. Rejecting this is rejecting his promises to you. Paul states in Philippians 4:13, *"I can do everything through Him who gives me strength."* This is a source of your strength to change those things that are wrong and to eliminate the need for blameshifting. There is no reason to look around you and say, "The reason I am not living my full Christian life is because..." In any of these situations:

Chronic lateness
Uncontrolled temper
Resentment
Unruly tongue
Unorganized home
Complaining
Alcoholism
Obesity
Envy
Negative attitude
Worry
Lack of discipline
Lack of knowledge
Moodiness
Timidity

or any other problem in your life, you can do what is necessary and right because God is giving you the strength.

Earlier in Philippians (2:13) Paul wrote, *"for it is God who works in you to will and to act according to his good purpose."* He is helping you not only to *do* right, he has promised to help you *want* to do what is right. When I realized that as a Christian I could ask for the will to do, it changed my whole outlook. I had prayed for so long, "help me to do what's right" and I didn't realize I could even pray, "Help me *want* to do what's right." The doing is easier when the wanting is straightened out.

Biblical Examples of Blameshifting

The very first interaction between humans involved blameshifting (Genesis 3:8-13). Adam and Eve started off their married life with blameshifting. When Satan had tempted Eve and she had succombed to his temptation, then in turn convinced Adam to sin also,

God came looking for them in the garden. The reply that Adam gave to God was, *"The woman you put here with me — she gave me some fruit from the tree, and I ate it."* Adam blamed Eve — and indirectly God — for his sin. God then turned to Eve and her reply also avoided her own sin. *"The serpent deceived me, and I ate."* Although both of them tried to point to another as responsible, they were not able to shift the punishment from themselves. God held each one, Adam, Eve, and the serpent guilty and responsible for his own part in the sin.

Cain followed the example he saw in his parents. In the next chapter of Genesis the story of his offering to God and that of his brother Abel is told. Abel's offering was acceptable to God, but Cain's was not. Rather than try to correct what was wrong in his life that made his sacrifice not acceptable, he turned to Abel, blaming him for the rejection, and killed him. When God confronted him with this murder, his reply was, *"Am I my brother's keeper?"* Again he refused to accept the blame that was rightly his. However, God as always was not turned away by the blameshifting, but held Cain responsible and punished him according to his sin.

In Jesus' parables of the New Testament he deals with the human tendency for blameshifting. He knows us so well. He gives us parables and lessons for every aspect that is a weakness in our lives.

The story of the great banquet (Luke 14:16-20) reveals ways men make excuses. The master was giving a feast and he invited men to come. But they each began making excuses. The first one said, *"I have just bought a field and I must go and see it."* The second one said, *"I have just bought five yoke of oxen and I'm on my way to try them out."* The third one said, *"I just got married and so I can't come."* One man was concerned with business, one concerned with agriculture, and finally one concerned with domestic problems. They did not come to the feast. Christ summed up that parable by saying that the master dismissed them and went out and found others. The invitation was withdrawn from those who blamed circumstances for not responding. God has no patience with excuse giving. When you begin giving excuses he will dismiss you just as the master in the parable. The reason is this: as long as you excuse your sin, you cannot overcome it.

In another parable (Luke 19:20,21) the blame was shifted to the master himself. The one-talent man, when the master came to him, said, *"I was afraid of you, because you are a hard man."* The reason he was not profitable, according to his statement, was that the master was hard and he was afraid of him. He was shifting the blame to the master. This was not accepted by the master as a legitimate reason for disobedience. The man was deprived of the opportunity he had wasted.

What Is Blamed?

A. Environment. Circumstances are most often blamed for shortcomings:

I am late because there was too much traffic.
It is too hot (or cold) for me to get out.
I don't have a nice enough house to be hospitable.
I was not feeling well that day so I lost my temper.
If I had what she does, I would be more generous.
I'm envious because I deserved that more than he did.
If you had arthritis, you would complain, too.

Often circumstances cannot be altered or controlled but your reaction to them can and must be channeled correctly.

"You can't control the length of your life, but you can control its width and depth. You can't control the countour of your countenance, but you can control its expression. You can't control the weather, but you can control the moral atmosphere that surrounds you. You can't control hard times or rainy days, but you can trust in Him who is able to see through both. You can't control the opportunities that others have, but you can grasp and use your own. Why worry about things you can't control, rather control the things that depend on you!"

Bill Swetmon

No one lives in a perfect environment. Even if you do have a situation conducive to Christian living there will be things that irritate, discourage, and hinder you. You must be able to control yourself in these situations rather than blaming the circumstances for your failure.

Another part of environment that we blame is the people around us — family, co-workers, social pressures, other Christians.

Often job pressures and peer pressure from co-workers are the reason given for the downfall of a Christian. Some working conditions do make Christianity difficult. However, it is your responsibility to either stand against those pressures or find another place to work. No job is worth the risk of losing faith in Christ or even falling short of the goal he has set for us.

Social pressure is another excuse given for sinning. Here is where Christians are lured into social drinking, young people tempted into sexual sins, and women fall into the trap of materialism. In his prayer for his followers Christ did not ask that the pressures of the world (social pressures) be removed but that they would be protected from these pressures: *"My prayer is not that you take them out of the world, but that you protect them from the evil one. They are not of the world, even as I am not of it."* (John 17:15,16)

Families are blamed for sinful reactions and for lack of service to Christ. How many times have you blamed your husband, your mother and father, your sisters and brothers, even your children for the sin in your own life. You are not able to significantly change any of those around you, but when you begin changing yourself, it is amazing how they will respond and become more Christ-like also. Instead of blaming them, try a different approach and watch the ripples of improvement radiate out from your efforts.

Sometimes even brothers and sisters in Christ are blamed. Elders, preachers, teachers, that kind Christian who has encouraged you also have shortcomings and weaknesses. If your Christianity is dependent upon another person; you will not be able to remain faithful. When a Christian sins it should not cause you to sin also. Although our brothers and sisters are a great encouragement to us, they are not our example. Christ is our example and he was perfect.

To follow anyone less than Christ is to be doomed to a lesser life.

B. Background. Common in today's society is the tendency to blame all of the idiosyncracies of personalities on parents even though parental influence may have ceased years ago. Your childhood has a great deal to do with the kind of person you are now, but it does not determine what you will be from now on. Part of maturity is being able to put behind childish things and to move on to adulthood. When childhood is used for an excuse for present behavior, then maturity has not been reached. Christ asks that each one determine his own course in adulthood. *"Therefore, my dear friends, as you have always obeyed...continue to work out your salvation with fear and trembling."* (Philippians 2:12)

C. God. The most misplaced blameshifting is done when God is accused of having been at fault. This is probably done most often and least recognized. Like Adam, people today say, *"You put...here..."* implying that God is responsible for the sin.

D. Satan. It is acceptable to blame all sins on the devil. Like Geraldine, we say, "The devil made me do it." The devil is tempting you, but in I Corinthians 10:13 we find, *"No temptation has seized you except what is common to man. And God is faithful; he will not let you be tempted beyond what you can bear. But when you are tempted, he will also provide a way out so that you can stand up under it."* When the devil is victorious in a life, it is because that person has not claimed this promise, either by desire to engage in that sin or by failing to seek the way out.

THE SOLUTION

1. Christian Reality Therapy. There is a method in psychology called reality therapy which probably comes the closest to being the Christian way of attacking this problem of blameshifting. Here are some steps taken from reality therapy and given a Christian emphasis.

Reality therapy just says, here is where you are today. Here are your problems. Now, what are you going to do about them? To determine this, you need to ask yourself some questions.

a. *What am I doing?* Be specific in listing the sins that are in your life. It does not help at this stage to try to decide *why* you are doing these things. When you begin looking for the whys, that leads right back into blameshifting. (I lose my temper *because* my children are unruly.)

b. *Is it pleasing to God? "Examine yourselves to see whether you are in the faith; test yourselves. Do you realize that Christ Jesus is in you — unless, of course, you fail the test?"* (2 Corinthians 13:5) It is necessary to examine your life and look at your behavior. Is it Christ-like? Hebrews 5:14 teaches that it is necessary to train your mind to discern good from evil. It is a matter of educating yourself in the ways of God (also Ephesians 5:15).

c. *How can I change?* Make a specific plan to change. Substitute a positive action or attitude for the sinful one. Ephesians 4:25-32 gives the best example of doing this. *"Put off falsehood"* and the substitute is *"speak truthfully."* Every time you take a negative trait out, you have to put a positive one in place of it. *"Be not angry"* is substituted with the positive *"do not let the sun go down while you are still angry."* Take action on the anger before it becomes permanent. *"He who is stealing must steal no longer."* However, that man must eat, so the positive is *"work, doing something useful with his own hands, so that he may have something to share with those in need."* Not only does this eliminate the stealing, but he even is able to help others along with himself. *"Do not let any unwholesome talk come out of your mouths"* is stopped by *"only what is helpful for building others up according to their needs, that it may benefit those who listen."* What can you substitute for the negatives in your life? This is your plan.

However, be sure the plan is not dependent upon anyone else. It needs to be *your* plan, one you can carry out alone. When you depend on another to help you carry it out, you will again be blameshifting if you are not successful. No matter what others may do, you are responsible for your actions. You cannot change those around you, only yourself.

d. *Am I committed to following the plan?* Unless you make a definite commitment, you will not continue following the plan. Realize that you *can* change (Philippians 4:13). Accept that you *must* change. *"Do not merely listen to the word, and so deceive yourselves. Do what it says."* (James 1:22)

2. Accept no excuses. Do not allow yourself to make excuses privately to yourself. Recognize the times you are looking for a scapegoat. For one week mark down on a piece of paper every time you hear yourself saying, "but" or "if" or other phrases that show blameshifting. You will be surprised how often you do this. Begin looking for the real culprit — your weakness — and work on it.

3. Realize God's promises. He has given some very specific promises that can help, and sometimes they are not accepted readily.

"Therefore, if anyone is in Christ, he is a new creation; the old has gone, the new has come!" (2 Corinthians 5:17) You no longer need to be encumbered with old sinful nature. When you see a sin that should have been put away with your old life, remember it does not have to be part of your new life. It can be buried.

"Therefore, we do not lose heart. Though outwardly we are wasting away, yet inwardly we are being renewed day by day." (2 Corinthians 4:16) Even though you fail, sometimes every day, each day brings a fresh opportunity to try again, strengthened by the day before. Just as you begin working on a sin it seems even harder to overcome. That may be because you are more aware of it, or it may be that the devil is working harder to keep you enslaved to it. However, as you are renewed every day in the inner strength that comes from God, you will be able to be victorious in the end in overcoming Satan's power over you in that sin.

"You, dear children, are from God and have overcome them, because the one who is in you is greater than the one who is in the world." (I John 4:4) You have power in you greater than any power without. Nothing in this world can overcome you if you remember to use the power of Christ who is in you.

DISCUSSION QUESTIONS·

1. Describe areas where you blameshift to those around you (family, co-workers, Christians, social pressure, etc.).

2. Why is blameshifting harmful?

3. Using a sin in your life, answer the questions under "Christian reality therapy." Does this provide a definite means of overcoming the sin?

4. Discuss God's promises to you that would help you overcome a sin so that blameshifting would not be necessary.

12. Selfishness

SELFISHNESS

the attitude others display when they won't let you have your way!

THE PROBLEM

Have you ever known something you should do (invite, visit or call someone) but you didn't? Have you ever realized you shouldn't buy something but you did? Have you ever wanted someone to do something so you made their life miserable until they did? If so, you have lost some battles to selfishness. When you lose a battle to selfishness, you do what *self* wants when *self* wants how *self* wants, even if it hurts others. Whether you realize it or not you are in a life and death struggle with selfishness. It started the day you were born and it will not end until the day you die.

It is the closest thing to original sin there is because you were born selfish. You came into the world demanding your way. You did not care what time of day or night, whether your mother was cold, tired, hungry or starving as long as you got what you wanted when you wanted it. However, in that selfishness you did not sin for your lack of knowledge, awareness and self-control kept you innocent. In fact, your selfishness was simply your natural man "uncontrolled," and he will battle to remain uncontrolled the rest of your life.

Satan Encourages Selfishness

Satan has been feeding your selfishness intraveneously every day of your life. He feeds it through TV commercials, radio programs, song lyrics, modern philosophy, etc. He is behind the current "Watch Out for Number One" philosophy so prominent in TV commercials, i.e., "It may cost more but I'm worth it...I owe it to myself...I do this for me...The most important person to me is me..." He makes it sound reasonable and logical.

Many other factors can also contribute to selfishness in your life. They do not make you selfish but they can create atmospheres where selfishness can flourish.

Battles with Selfishness

Your first battles with selfishness were fought for you by your parents. They fought by forcing you to share when you did not want to, compelling you to wait your turn when you demanded to be first, and making you consider others' welfare in your decisions.

Your second battles with selfishness were waged by peers in schoolrooms, on football fields, at roller skating rinks, at hamburger hangouts, etc. When selfishness was displayed in your life you were rebuffed until you either controlled it or learned to hide it.

The third battle is fought by family, friends, and business associates. It is fought in marital conflict, business deals, and family disagreements--all on the fields of serious consequence.

The fourth battle is yours alone. It must be fought on the couch of self-indulgence, on the field of manipulation, and in the auditorium of Number One. It must be fought every time you want to do something that will have an unhappy consequence or be inconsiderate of others.

The difficulty of your conflict will depend somewhat on the success of the first two battles. If your parents and peers waged successful battles against your selfishness, the next two may be nothing more than wars of containment. But if your selfishness responded to the first battles with stubbornness and rebellion, it probably commands a large portion of your life by now. And you may be experiencing conflict in many areas: family, friends, authorities, etc.

It is also possible you are being pressured by financial troubles, accumulated chores, and dog eat dog fights. For selfishness is at odds with the whole world and you are caught in the middle.

What Can You Do?

Know your enemy which is selfishness. Learn to recognize it in all its forms. For it is the basis of almost every sin in your life. You may hear such statements as, "Well, I may have trouble controlling my tongue but at least I am not selfish." Anytime you let an uncontrolled tongue, hurt others you are displaying selfishness. See it for what it is.

Think of Selfishness as Medusa, a goddess of Greek mythology. In place of hair her head was covered with hissing snakes. She seems to be a perfect illustration of selfishness if you visualize each hissing snake as a different sin growing out of selfishness. For example:

False Pride: If anything is self-centered, pride is. Even unselfish acts can be selfish when performed and savored for glory.

Sex: The misuse of sex is a primary act of selfishness, i.e., the man who demands his wife submit to his sexual desires regardless of her feelings, or the woman who selfishly withholds sex as a result of laziness, self-indulgence, inconsideration, or punishment. And certainly adultery and fornication are nothing more than uncontrolled selfish desires.

Greed: The most easily recognized form of selfishness. Greed takes what it has the power or advantage to get without regard for others.

Laziness: What is being lazy except doing what you want instead of what you should, which adds up to selfishness.

Irresponsibility: Every irresponsible act is certainly self-indulgence, a form of selfishness.

Uncontrolled Tongue: The tongue that lashes out and brings pain to others is rooted in a selfish heart.

Obvious selfishness is capable of controlling and destroying you. But even more dangerous is subtle selfishness. For example:

My Way: If a person is clever enough to subtly manipulate, it is usually an acceptable form of selfishness in our society.

Love: When selfishness controls your life, it produces a self-serving type of love based on possession and domination instead of sacrifice and giving.

Taking Advantage or Imposing—This is an abtruse form of selfishness and is usually practiced on people who are too kind to resist.

The different profiles of selfishness could go on forever. For everyone has a degree of selfishness and is usually very creative in the ways he displays it.

THE SOLUTION

How does God deal with selfishness? Through positive teaching with a "do it" method! In other words, he teaches you to overcome selfishness by teaching you to be *selfless*. He doesn't attempt to reason you out of selfishness, for selfishness is usually immune to reason. Instead he *works* you into *selflessness*.

An example of God's approach is 1 Timothy 6:17,18, *"Command those who are rich in this present world not to be arrogant nor to put their hope in wealth, which is so uncertain, but to put their hope in God, who richly provides us with everything for our enjoyment. Command them to do good, to be rich in good deeds, and to be generous and willing to share."* First, he teaches rich Christians where their hope and priorities are to be. Then he commands the "do its" to bring it about, i.e., do good, do be generous, do be willing to share.

Another example is Romans 15:1-3, *"We who are strong ought to bear with the failings of the weak and not to please ourselves. Each of us should please his neighbor for his good, to build him up. For even Christ did not please himself...."* Verse 1 tells you how

God wants you to be; verse 2 tells you what to do, and verse 3 tells you why.

There are many additional scriptures (Luke 3:11; 11:41; Ephesians 4:28; I Corinthians 10:24) in which God commands selflessness but submitting to them is often like the struggle one of our teenage daughters had. She was being scolded for some irresponsible behavior growing out of selfishness. We were pointing out that such behavior told us she wasn't grown up yet (a question she had been asking monthly). After a few minutes of miserable concentration she said, "It's just that some days my *want to's* are stronger than my *should do's.*" That is the state you are often in as you battle selfishness. However, God in his wisdom has provided Christians with a weapon for strengthening *should do's.*

Weapons for Battling Selfishness

The most powerful weapon against selfishness is *denial,* and it comes in several models. The model your parents used when they fought selfishness for you was called denial-by-parents. Your friends used the denial-by-peers. Society uses the denial-by-rules model. The one God provides for you is the denial-by-self, one of the most powerful, yet often most difficult versions of all.

An elementary use of denial-by-self would be: you *want* a new spring dress but your husband *needs* some new shirts and you haven't enough money for both. By getting the shirts for your husband you deny yourself something and selflessly give to someone else. That is striking a blow against selfishness.

Remember we compared selfishness to Medusa, a head covered with hissing snakes and each snake an aspect of selfishness. Everytime you deny yourself something for the good of someone else, you wound a snake on the head of selfishness. And as you weaken selfishness through your blows of denial, she loses much of her power to control your life. For you are strengthened through each denial and she is weakened.

Eventually the time will come that many of your blows will fall directly on the head of selfishness through denying self instead of just denying yourself something. For example, it's the evening of mid-week Bible study. You have had an exhausting day. You can tell you are going to get a headache. All you want to do is stay home and stare at the TV. But, you shake yourself, put on a smile and go to church, determined to be an excited student, upbuilding and encouraging to everyone you meet. Now you have landed a blow at the heart of all sin by denying *self*. There are many other ways.

The Ultimate Weapon

Denying yourself something and denying self are both defensive weapons against attacks of selfishness. But you cannot win a war with defensive measures alone. Instead you must take the battle to the heart of selfishness. That can only be done with the use of God's ultimate weapon; *self-sacrifice*. It is based on Romans 12:1-2 where we are taught to be *living sacrifices* to God. Being a living sacrifice is more than occasional acts of sacrifice. It is a planned lifestyle which is God-oriented. For example, it is a life that asks, "What can I do for God instead of what do I have to do for God?" It is the hand that reaches out to help instead of waiting to be grabbed. It is the heart that serves anytime not just when it is convenient. Ultimately, it is the life that is willing to be poured out like wine or broken like bread for God's sake.

Christ is a living sacrifice as described in Philippeans 2:6-8. He gave up what was rightfully his, took a position of service and accepted death at the hands of guilty men—all because he desired to please God. And God rewarded him richly according to verses 9 and 10.

The Spoils of War

In every war the spoils go to the victor. And your war with selfishness is no exception. If selfishness wins, your forfeit is your soul. On the other hand, if you overcome selfishness , you are promised a bounty beyond compare. God tells you in Luke 18:29-30, Matthew 19:29 and Mark 10:29 that no matter what you deny yourself for the sake of his Son and the gospel, you will receive a hundred times more in this life and eternal life in the age to come. In other words, *selflessness* has its reward. For no matter what you can obtain through *selfishness,* you can obtain a hundred times more through *selflessness.* Or as Jesus put it in John 12:25, *"The man who loves his life will lose it, while the man who hates his life in this world will keep it for eternal life."*

DISCUSSION QUESTIONS

1. What type of selfishness has been the most difficult for you to deal with?

2. Name some ways selfishness causes conflict. How? (James 3:13-16)

3. Name at least three atmospheres that contribute to selfishness.

4. Give two specific ways you can implement Philippians 2:3-4? What will you have to deny yourself to do so?

5. Read I Corinthians 13:4-8. How do the behaviors of love exemplify selflessness?

13. You Can Do It

"Examine yourselves to see whether you are in the faith; test yourselves. Do you not realize that Christ Jesus is in you—unless, of course, you fail the test?"

- 2 Corinthians 13:5

By this time you have overcome some of the sins you have been studying. However, you need to take time to evaluate where you stand in your Christian growth and where you need now to concentrate your efforts.

Football teams do this after each game. Even though they may have won, the films are viewed and each player criticizes himself to see what he could have done better, where he has improved over past times, and what areas need the most work for the future.

Some victories are easier than others, therefore they are not so much of a triumph. If a team is poor, standing last in the ratings, there is not much joy in beating them. If a sin is not much of a temptation to you, there is little triumph in not succumbing to it. On the other hand, a good team that is hard to beat provides a real challenge and it is a great victory, even if the score is very close. The same is true of sin. The sin that gives the most trouble provides the greatest joy when even a small victory is made to overcome it.

Repentance, Prayer, and Performance

Repentance, prayer, and, finally, performance are involved in overcoming any sin. Although they may not be mentioned in every chapter of this book, they definitely need to be a part of the solution in every chapter. Repentance of the sin turns you in the right direction. Prayer provides for forgiveness and strength in overcoming the sin. Performance—following thought on your resolve to conquer that sin—is the momentum that ultimately leads to victory.

These basic principles need to be understood clearly in order for progress to be made in Christian growth. Too often it is taken for granted that every Christian understands "repentance," when in fact it is a very hazy concept—one that has been heard all of his life, but never clearly explained. Also, the part of prayer in repenting and receiving forgiveness may be unclear. Finally, the role of living in a way that shows repentance may be confusing.

"Repent of this wickedness and pray to the Lord" was the admonition of Peter when he was talking with a man who had sinned (Acts 8:22). John told the religious men of that day to *"Produce fruit in keeping with repentance."* (Matthew 3:8). So repentance, prayer, and performance are all necessary in receiving forgiveness for the sins in your life and for endurance in conquering them.

Repentance

The Greek word for repentance (metanoia) literally means a change of mind. This is more than just sorrow. Often sorrow is expressed and really felt, but no resolve is made in regard to eliminating the sin for the future. However, sorrow is *part* of repentance, When one realizes the enormity of recrucifying Christ, heartfelt sorrow is inevitable. Each time a sin is brought to your attention, take a moment to picture Christ as he was on the cross and remember that in a sense, each sin crucifies him again (Hebrews 6:6). The pet-tiness of many sins is then seen—grumbling, anger, jealousy, resent-ment, and rebellion all lose their strong hold on your heart.

After sorrow must come a determination that this will not be part of your life in the future. Jesus expressed this to the woman brought to him when he said, *"Go now and leave your life of sin."* (John 8:11) Repentance has been described as a U-turn. Your life is turned in exactly the opposite direction from the sinful way it was directed. Perhaps in the subconcious mind there needs to be the command "about face" when temptations to sin come. *"Repent, then and turn to God, so that your sins may be wiped out, that times of refreshing may come from the Lord."* (Acts 3:19) Repentance is a *mind set* that results in a changed life.

Repentance must be accompanied by complete honesty in facing the sin. This honesty must be before God. It must also be with yourself and may even be at necessary at times with others. Only after facing the sin with honesty can the healing process begin. When there is a glossing over of the sin in the mind, the wound caused by it in your spiritual life continues to fester and irritate, even errupts again into another act of sinning.

Prayer

Just as Peter commanded "repent," he also included *"Pray to the Lord."* (Acts 8:22). This was a prayer asking forgiveness from the Lord. John teaches that you are deceitful if you claim to have no sin. But, *"If we confess our sins, he is faithful and just and will forgive us our sins and purify us from all unrighteousness."* (1 John 1:9) He continues, *"I write this to you that you will not sin. But if anybody does sin, we have one who speaks to the Father in our defense—Jesus Christ, the Righteous One."* (2:1) Along with repentance must come a prayer of confession, which results in forgiveness. It is so comforting to know that Jesus Christ himself will plead your case to the Father when this prayer is offered.

Prayer also provides strength to overcome the temptation to yield to that sin in the future. Just before his arrest, Jesus admonished his apostles with these words: *"Pray that you will not fall into temptation."* (Luke 22:40).

Performance

When Peter realized his sin in denying Christ, he repented of it. *"The Lord turned and looked straight at Peter. Then Peter remembered the word the Lord had spoken to him....And he went outside and wept bitterly."* (Luke 22:61, 62) But, unlike Judas who went out and hanged himself (Matthew 27:5), Peter spent his life in positive action for the Lord. Never again is there a record of his denying Christ. Rather, over and over he risked his life to proclaim Jesus as Christ, the Son of God. He truly *"produced fruit in keeping with repentance."* A person who has repented will live in such a way as to show his changed heart. The best way to overcome any sin is to substitute the opposite positive trait for it. This is, for a sinful tongue substitute good words; for worry, substitute trust; for uncontrolled anger substitute actions that correct the cause of your anger, etc.

SPIRITUAL MATURITY

One area where growth can be measured is spiritual maturity. Although this can cover many areas, three specific ones seem to be difficult for Christians.

1. *"Rejoice with those who rejoice; mourn with those who mourn."* (Romans 12:15) Often sharing sorrows is much easier than sharing joys. Even though there may be some awkwardness and uncertainty in how to express sympathy, usually the feeling comes freely. However, other sins may keep you from sharing joy. Pride, envy, jealousy, anger, bitterness, or resentment can prevent sincere rejoicing. If you cannot share joys it is time for a spiritual check to see which sin is getting in the way.

2. *"Do not be overcome by evil, but overcome evil with good."* (Romans 12:12) In present day language, this is acting instead of reacting. Many people spend their lives *bouncing off* situations. There is never any action taken until another first acts, then the result is most often a negative reaction. This permits another to have control of your life. Self control allows you to determine your actions regardless of the actions or attitudes of others. The glow of maturity shines brightly when this can be accomplished. There are daily opportunities to present a mature Christian attitude by acting instead of reacting in the home, in society, in business, sports, and school.

3. Tolerance is another attribute that shows development of spiritual maturity. One man has described tolerance as *conviction grown patient.* This is exactly right. Tolerance does not need to

indicate a lack of conviction. It does indicate understanding and patience with others.

There must be tolerance for the weak Christian. *"We who are strong ought to bear with the failings of the weak and not to please ourselves."* (Romans 15:1) Just as a mother is patient of her children's mistakes as they struggle to grow up, so mature Christians need to understand and encourage the weaker brother or sister. Allow them freedom to grow up in Christ. Often when one has overcome a sin in his life he is critical of those who are still struggling with it. This is self-righteousness and was strongly condemned by Christ.

There must also be tolerance for other's activities. *"It was he who gave some to be apostles, some to be prophets, some to be evangelists, and some to be pastors and teachers, to prepare God's people for works of service, so that the body of Christ may be built up until we all reach unity in the faith and in the knowledge of the Son of God and become mature, attaining to the whole measure of the fullness of Christ."* (Ephesians 4:11-13) *"We have different gifts according to the grace given us. If a man's gift is prophesying. let him use it in proportion to his faith. If it is serving, let him give generously; if it is leadership, let him govern diligently; if it is showing mercy, let him do it cheerfully."* (Romans 12:6-8)

Many times judgment is made based on man's value system rather than God's. Each one has something to contribute to the building up of the body. Sometimes others are labeled as less "spiritual" if they are involved in serving Christ in a different area. Although teaching is important and necessary, those not teaching may be performing just as vital a service. If you are engaged in going from door to door to spread the gospel, you are not more spiritual than the one who is using hospitality as a means to teach.

One beautiful eighty-year-old Christian woman spends hours making costumes, puppets, and other aids for the Bible school teachers to use. She has never taught a Bible class, yet her service is so valuable that the teachers would be handicapped without her help. She is not less spiritual because of the way she serves. Dorcas, Priscilla, and Lydia each received praise, but for different service. Dorcas clothed the poor, Priscilla taught, and Lydia showed hospitality.

PRESSING ON

Another area that needs to be evaluated is endurance. Noble beginnings are made daily, soon to be discarded when temptations come or when minor victories give a false sense of strength.

Along with Paul, Christians today need to say, *"I press on."* (Philippians 3:12:16) He was able to forget the past with its failures that discourage and its victories that tranquilize in view of reaching toward greater maturity and strength. He also recognized the difficulties encountered and the discipline required in making this a life-long effort.

He knew that he could reach this goal, however, because of where he was finding his strength. *"I can do everything through Him who gives me strength."* (Philippians 4:13) There is power in Christ, but without Him, there is nothing. *"I am the vine; you are the branches. If a man remains in me and I in him, he will bear much fruit; apart from me you can do nothing."* (John 15:5)

Paul also was able to claim for himself the blessings promised to Christians (1 Corinthians 10:13) Three facts are evident:

1) Temptations will come.
2) God will not allow more temptations than you can handle.
3) There will always be a way of escape.

Perhaps the best admonition is to KEEP ON KEEPING ON. The second mile is never crowded.

DISCUSSION QUESTIONS

1. What sin(s) is hardest for you to overcome? Have you made any progress in this area? How do you plan to proceed from here (outline a specific step-by-step program for overcoming this sin)?

2. Why are the abilities to rejoice with other Christians, positive reactions, and tolerance important in evaluating Christian maturity?

3. What motivates you to continue when you feel like giving up?

4. What is involved in repentance?

Other books for ladies' studies from 21st Century Christian....

Why Am I? by Charlotte Mize. Life is filled with both good and bad events. This study leads ladies to deal with what life offers in a God-pleasing manner and with a Christ-like attitude. 13 Lessons.

Batten Down the Hatches by Pat Scott. Great advice for handling the storms of life by a woman who has first-hand experience. She witnessed the murder of her husband, an elder in the church. Gripping! 8 lessons and a study guide.

Spiritual Seasons by Debbie Schmid. This sequel to *Spiritual Spring Cleaning* explores real-life challenges faced by many of today's Christian women. Schimd makes a powerful connection to scripture in each of the 13 lessons.